Carolyn Orr

7 - 4

A MANUAL FOR PROBLEM SOLVING IN BIBLE TRANSLATION

A MANUAL FOR PROBLEM SOLVING IN BIBLE TRANSLATION

MILDRED LARSON

THE SUMMER INSTITUTE OF LINGUISTICS
DALLAS, TEXAS

A Manual for Problem Solving in Bible Translation

Library of Congress Catalog Card Number 74–11863
ISBN 0–88312–917–5

First printing 1975 by Zondervan, Grand Rapids, MI
Second printing September 1975 by Zondervan

Printed in the United States of America.

CONTENTS

PREFACE

This manual is designed to develop basic skills through drill practice so that a student will not only easily recognize the different kinds of questions that face a translator but will also know the options available to resolve those questions. The training may be individual or in a classroom situation. Anyone using this material should first study carefully the text material which is found in Volumes 1 and 2 of this series. (Beekman, John, and Callow, John. 1974. *Translating the Word of God*. Grand Rapids, Michigan: Zondervan; and Callow, Kathleen. 1974. *Discourse Considerations in Translating the Word of God*. Grand Rapids, Michigan: Zondervan) These two books will be referred to as Beekman-Callow, 1974, and K. Callow, 1974, respectively in this third volume. Chapters 1-20 of this manual parallel the twenty chapters in the Beekman-Callow volume and chapters 21-25 the five chapters in the K. Callow volume.

Additional reading is also suggested at the beginning of each chapter. It is not essential to read the suggested material before doing the drills but it will broaden the background of the student on each topic if he does so. *The Bible Translator* and *Notes on Translation* have been especially helpful in providing bibliographical references and the student would do well to study many of these articles before doing the drills. Reference is also often made to the following three books: Nida, Eugene A. 1947. *Bible Translating*. New York: American Bible Society; Nida, Eugene A. 1964. *Toward a Science of Translating*. Leiden, the Netherlands: E. J. Brill; and Nida, Eugene A. and Taber, Charles R. 1969. *The Theory and Practice of Translation*, Leiden, the Netherlands: E. J. Brill. Throughout the bibliographical sections these five references will be referred to with the following abbreviations: *TBT; NOT;* Nida, 1947, Nida, 1964; and Nida and Taber, 1969.

An individual studying translation principles on his own should first read the pages in Beekman-Callow, 1974, and K. Callow, 1974, carefully. Having done this, he should be able to work through the drills applicable to the topic studied. An answer sheet will be available from the author. If the student finds he has not answered correctly, he should again read the text, looking for the reason for his misunderstanding.

In a classroom situation the teacher will want to be selective in the use of the drills. Since classes will vary in academic background from high school groups to graduate students, it will be up to the teacher to decide how much and which drill material to assign. The teacher may select only some of the drills related to a chapter or he may use all of the drills but assign only from three to five examples from each. Some of the drills are more useful for practice together as a class, others need careful study and must be worked on individually before there can be classroom discussion of the answers.

It cannot be overemphasized that these drills are for the purpose of learning principles of translation. They do not presuppose that each of the adjustments discussed will indeed be made in any given translation. The need of a particular change in the translation process will depend on the receptor language, i.e., the language into which one is translating. One should not assume that because a certain passage is used for drill purposes in this book it will therefore necessarily be changed in the same way in every translation.

Actually doing the drills will give the student practice in applying translation principles, but there is always the need to understand and to emphasize the translation theory that underlies each drill. In the broader context of theory and practice, the student learns to make judgments as to which, if any, changes need to be made in a specific situation.

It is hoped that the student, by focusing his attention on one type of translation problem at a time, will gain an awareness of the variety of problems facing a translator and thus be better prepared to anticipate and uncover problems as he begins his own translation program. It is also hoped that, having studied these materials before he begins his language analysis, he will be better prepared to collect the kinds of data that will be most helpful in making a meaningful, idiomatic translation of the Word of God into the receptor language.

Quotations of Scripture verses used in the drills follow the *Revised Standard Version* unless otherwise indicated. In many cases, only part of a verse is quoted, i.e., that part on which the drill focuses. No attempt has been made to distinguish those references that are quoted in full from those that are quoted in part.

The drills do not in all cases represent actual adjustments made in a specific language but do, however, represent the kinds of adjustments that have been found necessary again and again in various languages. Those adjustments in form which represent changes made in an actual translation were culled from the files of the Summer Institute of Linguistics in Mexico and Peru or from articles dealing with translation theory. The author is greatly indebted to John Beekman for the use of the files in Mexico in preparing these drills and also to her colleagues of the Wycliffe Bible Translators who supplied other material. Drill materials prepared by Katherine Barnwell and John Callow were especially helpful.

Some drills published in Larson, Mildred, L., 1965, "Drills on Linguistic Adjustments in Translation," *Notes on Translation with Drills*, edited by Beekman, John, Summer Institute of Linguistics, have been revised and included in this present volume. Additional drill material was prepared and published in tentative form in 1968. These sets of drills have been used in translation orientation courses and field workshops with much benefit to the students. However, they are now outdated. The final revision, which constitutes this volume, was further checked by use in Member-in-training Orientation Sessions for Wycliffe Bible Translators in 1973 and 1974.

Gratitude is due Eugenia Verigan, Eleanor McAlpine, and Alice Edmondson for typing the manuscript; Donald and Shirley Stewart and Betty Huizenga for reading the manuscript and making many helpful suggestions; and the following, who helped with proofreading: Gwen Longacre, Edna Jane Travis, Elaine Beekman, Dorothy Thomas, Joyce Overholt, and Nancy Graves.

The author is especially grateful to John Beekman for reading the entire text and making many helpful suggestions, and for his encouragement which made the completion of this book possible.

A MANUAL FOR
PROBLEM SOLVING IN
BIBLE TRANSLATION

CHAPTER 1

Idiomatic Versus Literal Translation

TEXT: Beekman-Callow, 1974, chapter 1

ADDITIONAL READING:

Beekman, John, 1965, "Idiomatic Versus Literal Translations," *NOT* 18:1-15

Beekman, John, 1966, " 'Literalism' a Hindrance to Understanding," *TBT* 17/4, 178-98

Bratcher, Robert G., 1958, "The Art of Translation," *TBT* 9/2, 84-89

Fox, David G., 1959, "How Intelligible is a Literal Translation?" *TBT* 10/4, 174-76

Nida, 1947, 11-30

Nida, Eugene A., 1959, "Principles of Translation as Exemplified by Bible Translating," *TBT* 10/3, 148-64

Nida, 1964, 11-29

Nida and Taber, 1969, 1-11

Nida, Eugene A., 1970, "Formal Correspondence in Translation," *TBT* 21/3, 105-13

Wonderly, William L., 1966, Bible Translations for Popular Use, London: United Bible Societies, 1-75

"Translations tend to cluster around two basic types — literal and idiomatic. . . . They . . . are scattered at varying points on the continuum between these two opposite poles. . . .

"A literal translation is characterized by a high transference of the linguistic *form* of the source language into the receptor language . . .

"On the other hand, an idiomatic translation aims at high transference of *meaning* from the source language into the receptor language . . ." (Beekman, 1965, 1, 2).

A. *Comparing literal and idiomatic translations.* Compare each of the following pairs of translations. Which one tends to be ~~more literal, which~~ more idiomatic? (The title of the version being quoted is not given, as it might influence the answer.)

Example: Matthew 3:15

    a) Thus it becometh us to fulfill all righteousness.

    b) We do well to conform in this way with all that God requires.

    ~~a is more literal~~, b is more idiomatic.

1) Matt. 3:8

    a) Bear fruit that befits repentance.

    b) Do the things that will show that you have turned from your sins.

2) Rom. 12:17

    a) If someone does evil to you, do not pay him back with evil. Try to do what all men consider to be good.

    b) Repay no one evil for evil, but take thought for what is noble in the sight of all.

3) 1 Cor. 15:20

    a) He has become the very first to rise of all who sleep the sleep of death.

    b) Christ has been raised from the dead, the first fruits of those who have fallen asleep.

4) James 3:13

    a) Who is wise and understanding among you? By his good life let him show his works in the meekness of wisdom.

    b) If there are any wise or learned men among you, let them show it by their good lives, with humility and wisdom in their actions.

5) Titus 2:13

    a) looking forward to that wonderful time we've been expecting, when his glory shall be seen — the glory of our great God and Savior, Jesus Christ.

    b) looking for the blessed hope and the appearing of the glory of our great God and Savior, Christ Jesus.

B. *Comparing various versions.* In each of the following, several versions are quoted. Classify the translations, telling in what order they would come along the continuum from highly literal to modified literal, to idiomatic, to unduly free. The passage is first quoted from Marshall's *Interlinear Greek-English New Testament*. The titles of the versions which follow are not given lest this information influence the answer.

Example: 1 Cor. 8:1: Now about the idolatrous sacrifices. . . .
 a) Now about working on Sunday. . . .
 b) Now concerning things offered to idols. . . .
 c) Now I will answer the question about food offered to idols. . . .
 d) Now in regard to food which has been offered to idols. . . .

b, d, c, a.

1) 1 Cor. 10:32: Without offence both to Jews be ye and to Greeks and to the church of God.   d, a, b, c
 a) Give no offence to Jews, or to Greeks, or to the church of God.
 b) So don't be a stumbling block to anyone, whether they are Jews or Gentiles or Christians.
 c) Set a good example for both whites and Negroes — for God's whole church.
 d) Give none offence, neither to the Jews, nor to the Greeks, nor to the Church of God.

2) Rom. 16:16: Greet one another with kiss a holy.   b, c, a, d
 a) Shake hands warmly with each other.
 b) Salute one another with a holy kiss.
 c) Greet one another with the kiss of peace.
 d) Give one another a hearty handshake all around for my sake.

3) Luke 20:47: who devour the houses of the widows.   c, a, d, b
 a) who swallow the property of widows.
 b) they are planning schemes to cheat widows out of their property.
 c) who devour widows' houses.
 d) who take advantage of widows and rob them of their homes.

4) Rom. 8:12: So then, brothers, debtors we are, not to the flesh according to flesh to live.   e, b, a, c, d
 a) So, brothers, we are under obligation, but not to the physical nature, to live under its control.

b) So, then, my brethren, we have a duty, but it is not to the flesh: it is not to live according to the flesh.

c) So, dear brothers, you have no obligations whatever to your old sinful nature to do what it begs you to do.

d) It follows, my friends, that our lower nature has no claim upon us; we are not obliged to live on that level.

e) Therefore, brothers, we are debtors — but not to the flesh, to live according to the flesh.

5) Acts 7:38: This is the one having been in the church in the desert with the angel speaking to him in the Mount Sinai and with the fathers of us, who received oracles living to give to you.   e, a, c, d, b

a) He it was who, when they were assembled there in the desert, conversed with the angel who spoke to him on Mount Sinai, and with our forefathers; he received the living utterances of God, to pass on to us.

b) How true this proved to be, for in the wilderness, Moses was the go-between — the mediator between the people of Israel and the Angel who gave them the Law of God — the Living Word — on Mount Sinai.

c) He is the one who was with the people of Israel assembled in the desert; he was there with our ancestors and with the angel who spoke to him on Mount Sinai; he received God's living messages to pass on to us.

d) This is the one who in the desert church was go-between with the Angel who spoke to him on Mount Sinai, and with our forefathers; he received the living word to impart to us.

e) This is he, that was in the church in the wilderness with the Angel which spake to him in the Mount Sinai, and with our fathers: who received the lively oracles to give unto us.

CHAPTER 2

Fidelity in Translation

TEXT: Beekman-Callow, 1974, chapter 2

ADDITIONAL READING:

Grimes, Joseph E., 1963, "Measuring 'Naturalness' in a Translation," *TBT* 14/2, 49-62

Grimes, Joseph E., 1968, "Fidelity in Translation," *TBT* 19/4, 164-66

Gudschinsky, Sarah C., 1967, "Frequency Counts, Naturalness, and Style," *NOT* 28:13-14

Larson, Mildred L., 1967, "The Relationship of Frequency Counts and Function," *NOT* 28:14-16

Moore, Bruce R., 1964, "Second Thoughts on Measuring 'Naturalness,'" *TBT* 15/2, 83-87

Nida, Eugene A., 1950, "Translation or Paraphrase," *TBT* 1/3, 97-106

Nida, 1964, 156-92

Nida and Taber, 1969, 12-32

Phillips, J. B., 1958, "Translator's Foreword," *The New Testament in Modern English*, vii-x

Robinson, Dow F., 1963, "Native Texts and Frequency Counts as Aids to the Translator," *TBT* 14/2, 63-71

Trinklein, Michael, 1970, "Luther's Insights into the Translator's Task," *TBT* 21/2, 80-88

Wonderly, William L., 1964, "Some Factors of Meaningfulness," *TBT* 14/3, 114-25

"A translation which transfers the meaning and the dynamics of the original text is to be regarded as a faithful translation. . . .

"The question of fidelity thus comes down to the two questions:

21

(1) Does the translation communicate the same meaning as the original? (2) Does it communicate it as clearly and as idiomatically as the original did? If the answer to these two questions is yes, then it has every right to be called a 'faithful translation'" (Beekman-Callow, 1974, 31, 32).

A. *Identifying historical and didactic passages.* The source material to be translated may be classed as historical or didactic. Some passages consist of both types of material interwoven within the passage. Study the passage in which each of the following occur and decide if it is (1) primarily a historical account, (2) primarily a didactic passage, or (3) involves both historical and didactic material.

1) Mark 1:6
   Now John was clothed with camel's hair, and had a leather girdle around his waist.

2) Luke 17:2
   It would be better for him if a millstone were hung round his neck and he were cast into the sea, than that he should cause one of these little ones to sin.

3) Mark 6:8-9
   He charged them to take nothing for their journey except a staff; no bread, no bag, no money in their belts; but to wear sandals and not to put on two tunics.

4) Luke 6:29
   To him who strikes you on the cheek, offer the other also; and from him who takes away your cloak do not withhold your coat as well.

5) Luke 6:40
   A disciple is not above his teacher, but every one when he is fully taught will be like his teacher.

6) Mark 4:7
   Other seed fell among thorns and the thorns grew up and choked it, and it yielded no grain.

7) Luke 6:44
   Each tree is known by its own fruit. For figs are not gathered from thorns, nor are grapes picked from a bramble bush.

8) Matt. 21:19

And seeing a fig tree by the wayside he went to it, and found nothing on it but leaves only.

9) Matt. 24:32

From the fig tree learn its lesson: as soon as its branch becomes tender and puts forth its leaves, you know that summer is near.

10) Luke 13:6

And he told this parable: "A man had a fig tree planted in his vineyard; and he came seeking fruit on it and found none.

B. *Application to "figs."* In numbers 7-10 above, *figs* are mentioned. Assume you are translating into a language which has no word for fig. In which of these passages would it be necessary to translate with a phrase that would distinguish the tree as being a *fig* tree? In which would some more generic word such as *tree, fruit,* or *fruit tree* be acceptable as a lexical equivalent?

C. *Identifying naturalness.* A faithful translation must communicate the same meaning as the original. At the same time it must communicate clearly. Which of the two passages compared seems to you to communicate more clearly? What differences between the passages makes one easier to understand than the other(s)?

1) Luke 7:44

     a) I entered your house, you gave me no water for my feet. (RSV)

     b) I came into your house but you provided no water to wash my feet. (*Phillips*)

2) Luke 18:13

     a) But the tax collector, standing far off, would not even lift his eyes to heaven, but beat his breast, saying, "God, be merciful to me a sinner!" (RSV)

     b) But the corrupt tax collector stood at a distance and dared not even lift his eyes to heaven, but beat his chest in sorrow, exclaiming, "God, be merciful to me, a sinner." (LB)

3) Mark 12:14

     a) Tell us, is it against our Law to pay taxes to the Roman Emperor? Should we pay them, or not? (TEV)

     b) Is it right to pay taxes to Caesar or not? (*Moffatt*)

4) Mark 1:2
   a) It began as the prophet Isaiah had written: " 'Here is my messenger,' says God; 'I will send him ahead of you to open the way for you.' " (TEV)
   b) As it it written in Isaiah the Prophet, 'See, I am sending my messenger before thy face, who will prepare thy way.' (*Weymouth*)

5) 1 Cor. 10:1
   a) Our fathers all passed through the sea. (RSV)
   b) Our ancestors all passed through the Red Sea. (NEB)
   c) Our ancestors who followed Moses all passed safely through the Red Sea. (TEV)

6) Luke 12:5
   a) I will show you whom to fear: fear God who, after killing, has the authority to throw into hell. (TEV)
   b) But I will warn you whom to fear: fear him who, after he has killed, has power to cast into hell. (RSV)

7) Matt. 22:32
   a) 'I am the God of Abraham, and the God of Isaac, and the God of Jacob.' He is not God of the dead, but of the living. (RSV)
   b) 'I am the God of Abraham, and I am the God of Isaac, and I am the God of Jacob.' Since God is now the God of those ancestors of ours, it means that they are not just dead bodies, they still have life. (*Aguaruna*)

8) Rom. 3:27
   a) So what becomes of our boasts? There is no room for them. What sort of law excludes them? The sort of law that tells us what to do? On the contrary, it is the law of faith, since, as we see it, a man is justified by faith and not by doing something the Law tells him to do. (*Jerusalem Bible*)
   b) Where then is there room for boasting? It is shut out. On what principle? On that of merit? No, but on the principle of faith. For we deem that a man is accounted righteous by faith, apart from fulfillment of the Law. (*Weymouth*)

9) Luke 17:26
   a) As it was in the days of Noah, so will it be in the days of the Son of man. (RSV)

b) In the time of the coming of the Son of Man, life will be as it was in the days of Noah. (*Phillips*) *→ changes order of clauses.*

10) Rom. 2:4

a) Do you think so little of the wealth of God's kindness and patience and long-suffering? Can you not see that the kindness of God should lead you to repentance? (*Williams*)

b) Don't you realize how patient he is being with you? Or don't you care? Can't you see that he has been waiting all this time without punishing you, to give you time to turn from your sin? His kindness is meant to lead you to repentance. (LB) *chg. lexical items + adds summary statement*

D. *Historical fidelity.* In the following drills the RSV is compared with the Koinonia "Cotton Patch" Version, which contains violations of historical fidelity. Identify these historical inaccuracies.

Example: 1 Cor. 1:2

a) To the church of God which is at Corinth, to those sanctified in Christ Jesus.

b) To God's people in Atlanta — those whom Jesus Christ has set apart by calling them together.
Atlanta — violates the historical fact that Paul wrote to the people in *Corinth*.

1) 1 Cor. 1:13

a) Is Christ divided? Was Paul crucified for you? Or were you baptized in the name of Paul? *ok*

b) Tell me this, since when did Christ get so split up? And was Paul lynched for you? Or were you given Paul's name when you were initiated? *only in generic sense.*

2) 1 Cor. 1:19

a) For it is written, "I will destroy the wisdom of the wise, and the cleverness of the clever I will thwart."

b) It's just like the Scripture says, "I will tear to bits the dissertations of the Ph.D.s; I will pull the rug from under those who have all the answers." *ok. For 'thwart'*

3) 1 Cor. 3:2

a) I fed you with milk, not solid food; for you were not ready for it; and even yet you are not ready.

b) I gave you a bottle, not solid food. That's all you could take. And you still don't seem to be doing much better.

4) 1 Cor. 8:5, 6

    a) For although there may be so-called gods in heaven or on earth — as indeed there are many "gods" and many "lords" — yet for us there is one God, the Father, from whom are all things and for whom we exist.

    b) Even though there are also many special days on both Catholic and Protestant calendars, such as those to saints and special events, still for us God alone is supreme, our Father, the source of all things. We are his. *ok if not referring to salvation*

5) 1 Cor. 16:1

    a) Now concerning the contribution for the saints: as I directed the churches of Galatia, so you also are to do.

    b) Now a few words about that fund for sharing with the church members. I'd like for you all to follow the same plan I recommended to the Alabama churches.

E. *Accuracy of meaning.* Following the quotations from RSV, a proposed translation is given for each verse. These are not published translations but made up to illustrate this topic. Check each verse carefully to see if it has (1) incomplete information, (2) extraneous information, or (3) different information. Explain.

Example: Acts 2:37

    a) Now when they heard this they were cut to the heart, and said to Peter and the rest of the apostles, "Brethren, what shall we do?"

    b) When the people heard this, they were deeply troubled, and they said to Peter, "What shall we do, brothers?" incomplete — "rest of the apostles" is not included.

1) John 17:9

    a) I am praying for them; I am not praying for the world but for those whom thou has given me, for they are thine.

    b) I am praying for those who are mine. I'm not praying for the other people in the world. I'm just praying for those who are mine, for they are thine. *incomplete*

2) Acts 8:36

    a) And as they went along the road they came to some water, and the eunuch said, "See, here is water! What is to prevent my being baptized?"

    b) When Philip finished speaking, and the chariot came

along some water the eunuch said, "Look, there is some water here! Could I be baptized now?"

3) Acts 6:10
   a) But they could not withstand the wisdom and the Spirit with which he spoke.
   b) Stephen spoke with the power of the Holy Spirit and the people were amazed at what he said.

4) Acts 1:12
   a) Then they returned to Jerusalem from the mount called Olivet, which is near Jerusalem, a sabbath day's journey away.
   b) They left the mount called Olivet and returned to Jerusalem which was near-by, as far as they were able to walk on the rest day.

5) Acts 5:7
   a) After an interval of about three hours his wife came in, not knowing what had happened.
   b) Three hours after they carried Ananias out his wife came running in. She didn't know that her husband had died.

F. *Comparing versions.* Compare the following translations of Galatians 4:24-26. Which translation do you feel expresses the accurate meaning most clearly? In light of the principles of fidelity in translation, do you think any of the translations given are not faithful translations in every detail? State your reasons.

1) Which things are an allegory: for these are the two covenants; the one from the mount Sinai, which gendereth to bondage, which is Agar. For this Agar is mount Sinai in Arabia, and answereth to Jerusalem which now is, and is in bondage with her children. But Jerusalem which is above is free, which is the mother of us all. (KJV)

2) Now this is an allegory: these women are two covenants. One is from Mount Sinai, bearing children for slavery; she is Hagar. Now Hagar is Mount Sinai in Arabia; she corresponds to the present Jerusalem, for she is in slavery with her children. But the Jerusalem above is free, and she is our mother. (RSV)

3) There is a hidden meaning here. Those two women stand for the two covenants. One of the women, Hagar, stands

for the covenant which God made long ago on Mount Sinai.
Hagar was a slave, and her children were born into slavery.
So Hagar stands for Mount Sinai, and also for the present-
day town of Jerusalem, because Jerusalem and all her people are in slavery. But the real town of God, that is, Jerusalem above, is not in slavery. That is the place to which
we belong. (hypothetical)

added

deletes "Arabia"

good

4) Now this true story is an illustration of God's two ways of
helping people. One way was by giving them his laws to
obey. He did this on Mount Sinai, when he gave the Ten
Commandments to Moses. Mount Sinai, by the way, is
called "Mount Hagar" by the Arabs — and in my illustration Abraham's slave-wife Hagar represents Jerusalem, the
mother-city of the Jews, the center of that system of trying
to please God by trying to obey the Commandments; and
the Jews, who try to follow that system, are her slave children. But our mother-city is the heavenly Jerusalem, and
she is not a slave to Jewish Laws. (LB)

clearer for a
new reader but
maybe some of
this needs to be
in a Bible Teaching
book.

5) This can be regarded as an allegory. Here are the two
agreements represented by the two women: the one from
Mount Sinai bearing children into slavery, typified by
Hagar (Mount Sinai being in Arabia, the land of the descen-
dents of Ishmael, Hagar's son), and corresponding to pres-
ent-day Jerusalem — for the Jews are still, spiritually
speaking, "slaves." But the free woman typifies the heavenly Jerusalem, which is the mother of us all, and is spiritually "free." (*Phillips*)

makes the allegory's
meaning clearer

CHAPTER 3

Implicit and Explicit Information

Text: Beekman-Callow, 1974, chapter 3

Additional Reading:

Beekman, John, 1968, "Implicit Information in Translation," *NOT* 30:3-13

Ballard, D. Lee, and Pallesen, Kemp, 1974, *NOT* 51:31-35

Larson, Mildred L., 1969, "Making Explicit Information Implicit in Translation," *NOT* 33:15-20

Nida, 1964, 227-29

Nida and Taber, 1969, 115

Taber, Charles R., 1970, "Explicit and Implicit Information in Translation," *TBT* 21/1, 1-9

Taber, Charles R., 1972, "Why Don't Writers Say Everything," *TBT*, 23/2, 207-11   *Yeah!*

A. *Ellipsis.* "Though ellipsis occurs in all languages, the particular structures which permit such 'omitted' words are by no means identical from language to language. Accordingly, in an expression almost obligatorily elliptical in one language, an ellipsis may not be permitted in another. Hence, a clause such as 'he is greater than I' may require expansion into 'he is greater than I am great' " (Nida, 1964, 227).

For many passages in which ellipses must be filled out in the translation the parallelism of the structure supplies the information needed to fill out the ellipses, as in the illustration given above. In the following there are similar ellipses which often must be filled out. Rewrite filling out the elliptical expression.

Example: Matt. 26:5
But they said, "Not during the feast, lest there be a tumult among the people."

But they said, "Let's not arrest him during the feast, lest there be a tumult among the people."

1) Mark 6:38

   And he said to them, "How many loaves have you? Go and see." And when they had found out, they said, "Five, and two fish."

2) Mark 12:27

   He is not the God of the dead, but of the living.

3) John 1:21

   And they asked him, "What then? Are you Elijah?" He said, "I am not."

4) John 2:10

   He said to him, "Every man serves the good wine first; and when men have drunk freely, then the poor wine."

5) John 4:12

   Jacob, who gave us the well, and drank from it himself, and his sons, and his cattle.

6) John 7:46

   "No man ever spoke like this man!"

7) 1 Cor. 2:8

   None of the rulers of this age understand this, for if they had, they would not have crucified the Lord of glory.

8) 1 Cor. 7:35

   I say this not to lay any restraint upon you, but to promote good order.

B. *Linguistically obligatory additions.* Often the language into which one is translating demands that information be made explicit to avoid wrong meanings, but there is not an easy parallelism from which to find what must be added. However, the context of the sentence itself or of the entire passage may give the information. Some verbs require that an object be made explicit in order to avoid wrong meaning, others require a location, etc. In each of the following the passage is given and then a note as to what is required by the receptor language. What addition would you make to fulfill this requirement? Base your answer on the context.

Example: Acts 5:16
The people also gathered . . . bringing the sick and those
afflicted with unclean spirits, and they were all healed.
In Cuicateco, *healed* can be used only to talk about *sick-
ness*, not to talk about *casting out evil spirits*. To be sure
that these people were helped as well, the translators had
to make an obligatory addition. It now reads: . . . all of
them were healed and the evil spirits left them.

1) Acts 16:11, 12
We made a direct voyage to Samothrace, and the following
day to Neapolis, and from there to Philippi. (In a language
that never has a clause consisting of only time and location
what verb would you add in the last two clauses?)

2) Matt. 26:6
in the house of Simon the leper (Without an addition this
would mean that Simon was not yet cured of leprosy. What
modification would you add to *leper?*)

3) John 4:20
Our fathers worshiped in this mountain: and you say that
Jerusalem is the place where men ought to worship. (The
verb *worship* requires an object.)

4) Mark 1:21
And they went into Capernaum, and immediately on the
sabbath he entered the synagogue. (If translated literally
it means that the disciples did not go to the synagogue.)

5) 1 Cor. 7:26
I think that in view of the impending distress, it is well for
a person to remain as he is. (*Remain* when used by itself
about people can only mean to stay in one place. What
addition is needed to give the right meaning *to remain?*)

6) Mark 8:20
"And the seven for the four thousand, how many baskets
full of broken pieces did you take up?" (Numbers that are
attributives occur only as modifiers. Add the nouns that
they modify. Check the context.)

C. *Omitted chronological sequences.* "In reporting any happening which involves a sequence of events, it is unlikely that all of

the events will be told in detail. Some will be left implicit. When translating from one language to another, the events selected by the original author for specific mention may be too few" (Beekman, 1968, 7).

For example, in John 1:43 — "The next day Jesus decided to go to Galilee. And he found Philip . . ." — Aguaruna had to add the information that Jesus went. "The next day Jesus, wanting to, he went to Galilee. Having done so, he saw Philip . . . ."

Study the following to see what implied action would probably need to be added in some translations to make the story clear. Rewrite the passage, making explicit this implied action.

> Example: Acts 14:19, 20
> They stoned Paul and dragged him out of the city, supposing that he was dead. But when the disciples gathered about him . . . .
>
> They stoned Paul and dragged him out of the city. Supposing that he was dead, they left him. But when the disciples arrived, they gathered about him . . . .

1) Matt. 2:7
   Then Herod summoned the wise men secretly and ascertained from them what time the star appeared.

2) John 2:9, 10
   The steward of the feast called the bridegroom and said to him . . . .

3) John 4:28
   So the woman left her water jar, and went away into the city, and said to the people . . . .

4) John 6:10
   Jesus said, "Make the people sit down." Now there was much grass in the place; so the men sat down, in number about five thousand.

5) Acts 5:10
   When the young men came in, they found her dead, and they carried her out and buried her beside her husband.

6) Acts 9:1, 2
   Saul went to the high priest and asked him for letters to the synagogues at Damascus, so that he might bring them bound to Jerusalem.

7) Acts 20:1, 2
Paul took leave of them and departed for Macedonia. When he had gone through these parts he came to Greece.

8) Acts 20:5
These went on and were waiting for us at Troas.

D. *Omitted main clause with reason clauses.* In a number of passages the reason clause is stated but the main clause is only implied, often being carried by the word "for." For example, Matthew 2:2: "Where is he who has been born king of the Jews? For we have seen his star." The word "for" implies the main clause — "we know that he has been born." In Aguaruna this verse is translated "Where is the one who has been born, the one who will rule the people of Judea? We know he has been born because we saw the star."

Rewrite the following, making explicit the main clause, which is only implied in the source language. You will need to study the context.

1) Matt. 16:7
And they discussed it among themselves, saying, "[For] we brought no bread."

2) Matt. 2:20
"Rise, take the child and his mother, and go to the land of Israel, for those who sought the child's life are dead."

3) Matt. 4:6
If you are the Son of God, throw yourself down; for it is written, 'He shall give his angels charge of you.'

4) Mark 3:29, 30
Whoever blasphemes against the Holy Spirit never has forgiveness, but is guilty of an eternal sin — for they said, "He has an unclean spirit."

5) Acts 21:13
Then Paul answered, "What are you doing, weeping and breaking my heart? For I am ready not only to be imprisoned but even to die at Jerusalem for the name of the Lord Jesus."

6) Acts 23:5
"I did not know, brethren, that he was the high priest; for it

is written, 'You shall not speak evil of a ruler of your people.'"

7) John 4:9
The Samaritan woman said to him, "How is it that you, a Jew, ask a drink of me, a woman of Samaria?" For the Jews have no dealings with Samaritans.

E. *Making information explicit.* In the following the item that is to be made explicit is given in parentheses following the passage. Rewrite adding this information.

Example: James 2:24
You see that a man is justified by works and not by faith alone. (contrast implied by alone)
You see that a man is justified by faith shown by his works and he is not justified by faith alone.

1) Mark 5:41
He said to her, "Talitha cumi"; which means, "Little girl, I say to you, arise." (source or language of the foreign words)

2) James 1:5
If any of you lacks wisdom, let him ask God who gives to all men generously and without reproaching, and it will be given him. (condition clause to go with final main clause)

3) Acts 6:6
These they set before the apostles, and they prayed and laid their hands upon them. (purpose of this action)

4) Mark 7:32
They besought him to lay his hands upon him. (purpose of this action)

F. *Old Testament quotations.* The information given in the introduction of an OT quotation may need to be expanded to make explicit the writer, speaker, or persons spoken to in order to avoid wrong meaning or ambiguities that are confusing to the reader. For example, Mark 1:2 says, "As it is written in Isaiah the prophet, 'Behold I send my messenger . . . .'" Unless the information that God is the speaker is added, the impression may be left that Isaiah himself is sending the messenger. And so the verse might be translated, "As the prophet Isaiah wrote, 'God said, "Behold, I send my messenger . . . ."'"

For each of the following quotations used in the NT the reference in the OT is also given. Study each passage to determine if information concerning the speaker, writer, or persons spoken to needs to be added to avoid potential wrong meaning. Check the OT reference in order to supply this information where needed. Rewrite only those verses in which you see a possible need for making explicit one or more of these participants.

Example: Matt. 4:4
But he answered, "It is written, 'Man shall not live by bread alone.' " (Deut. 8:3)
But he answered, "Moses wrote that God said, 'Man shall not live by bread alone.' "

1) Matt. 5:21
You have heard it was said to the men of old, "You shall not kill." (Exod. 20:13)

2) Matt. 5:31
It was also said, "Whoever divorces his wife, let him give her a certificate of divorce." (Deut. 24:1)

3) Matt. 7:23
And then I will declare to them, "I never knew you; depart from me, you evil doers." (Ps. 6:8)

4) Matt. 12:7
And if you had known what this means, "I desire mercy, and not sacrifice." (Hos. 6:6)

5) Matt. 12:17, 18
This was to fulfill what was spoken by the prophet Isaiah: "Behold, my servant whom I have chosen, . . . I will put my spirit upon him." (Isa. 42:1-3)

6) Matt. 15:7
You hypocrites! Well did Isaiah prophesy of you, when he said: "This people honors me with their lips." (Isa. 29:13)

7) Matt. 21:4, 5
This took place to fulfill what was spoken by the prophet saying, "Tell the daughter of Zion . . . ." (Isa. 62:11)

8) Matt. 21:16
And Jesus said to them, "Yes, have you never read, 'Out of

the mouth of babes and sucklings thou has brought perfect praise'?" (Ps. 8:2)

9) Matt. 22:31, 32
And as for the resurrection of the dead, have you not read what was said to you by God, "I am the God of Abraham, and the God of Isaac . . . ." (Exod. 3:6)

10) Matt. 26:31
Then Jesus said to them, "You will all fall away because of me this night; for it is written, 'I will strike the shepherd, and the sheep of the flock will be scattered.'" (Zech. 13:7)

G. *Review.* The following is a literal word-for-word back translation of Acts 16:11-15 in a Nigerian language. Compare this back translation carefully with the *Revised Standard Version* or *American Standard Version* of this passage. Mark any information that was implicit in the rsv but which has been made explicit in the translation. Explain in each instance why you think the information has been made explicit.

[11]We got-into boat, got-up left from Troas, went straight travelled crossed the big-river, until we came reached to Samothrace. When next-day came, we again travelled, came landed at Neapolis. [12]We got-up left from Neapolis, we walked by land, came reached to Philippi, which is the foremost-town in the region of Macedonia. It is also the place where the people of Rome made a settlement. We stayed in that town for a few days. [13]It came reached to the Resting-day, we went outside the town, walked to river-side-bank, because we thought that the Jews would come gather in that place pray. When we reached there we sat seat there, we spoke word with some women who had come gathered there. [14]In the midst of those women who listened to our words, a certain person was there who was called Lydia, who was a person who was-habitually-selling red-cloth. That woman, she-came from Thyatira, she-was-habitually-worshiping God. God opened her heart so that she should repair ear listen to words of Paul. [15]She and all her people, they came baptized water. Then she called us to her house, she said thus, "If you think that I place the Lord Jesus as true (i.e., believe truly in the Lord Jesus), come stay at my house." She persuaded us that we should go there.

CHAPTER 4

Analyzing the Components of Meaning in a Word, Part 1

TEXT: Beekman-Callow, 1974, chapter 4

ADDITIONAL READING:

Bendix, Edward Herman, 1966, "Componential Analysis of General Vocabulary: The semantic structure of verbs in English, Hindi, and Japanese," *International Journal of American Linguistics,* Part II, 32:2, 1-190

Elkins, Richard, 1971, "The Structure of Some Semantic Sets of W. B. Manobo," *NOT* 41:10-15

Frake, Charles O., 1961, "The Diagnosis of Disease Among the Subanun of Mindanao," *American Anthropologist,* 63:113-32

Glover, Mr. & Mrs. Maurice, 1972, "Upon the Green Grass," *NOT* 46:26-27

Lauriault, James, 1951, "Lexical Problems in Shipibo Mark," *TBT,* 2/2, 56-66

Lounsbury, Floyd G., 1965, "A Semantic Analysis of the Pawnee Kinship Usage," *Language* 32, 158-94

Manson, Richard, 1971, "Understanding the World of the Supernatural," *NOT* 39:3-12

Moore, Bruce R., 1973, "Semantic Components of Geometric Planes," *NOT* 49:18-21

Nida, Eugene A., 1961, "Some Problems of Semantic Structure and Translational Equivalence," in *A William Cameron Townsend en el XXV Aniversario del Instituto Lingüístico de Verano,* (Cuernavaca, Mexico: Tipográfica Indígena)

Nida, 1964, 37-93

Nida and Taber, 1969, 56-90

Olson, Ronald D., 1968, "Lexical Equivalence and Semantic Components," *NOT* 29:15-20

Pike, Eunice V., 1967, "Skewing of the Lexical and Grammatical Hierarchies as It Affects Translation," *NOT* 23:1-3

Ullman, Stephen, 1962, *Semantics, An Introduction to the Science of Meaning,* (Oxford: Basil Blackwell)

Ullman, Stephen, 1963, "Semantic Universals," *Universals in Language,* ed. Greenberg, Cambridge: M.I.T. Press, 172-207

Wallace, Anthony F. C., and Atkins, John, 1960, "Meaning of Kin Terms," *American Anthropologist,* 62:1, 58-80

A. *Identifying the semantic class of a word.* Words are divided into four semantic classes: Things, Events, Abstractions, and Relations. To which class does each of the italicized words belong? Some may include more than one class.

Example: Col. 1:4
We have heard of *your faith in* Christ *Jesus.*
we —Thing; your — Relation, Thing; faith — Event; in — Relation; Jesus — Thing

1) Matt. 3:8
Bear fruit that befits *repentance.*

2) Matt. 5:7
Blessed are the *merciful,* for they shall obtain *mercy.*

3) Mark 9:29
This kind cannot be driven out by anything but *prayer.*

4) Luke 23:22
Why what *evil* has he done? *I* have found *in* him no *crime* deserving death.

5) John 11:4
This *illness* is not unto *death*; it is for the *glory* of God.

6) Acts 9:12
so *that* he might regain his *sight*

7) Acts 13:38
Through this man *forgiveness of sins* is proclaimed to *you.*

8) Rom. 2:4

Do you not know *that* God's *kindness* is meant to lead *you* to repentance?

9) 2 Cor. 5:19

not counting their *trespasses* against *them,* and entrusting to us the *message* of *reconcilation*

10) Col. 1:14

in *whom* we have *redemption*

B. *Matching semantic and grammatical classes.* In each of the following, determine the semantic class or classes of the words in italics. Then rewrite the portion of the verse given, using a grammatical part of speech that corresponds to the semantic class you have given to the italicized word. Use the active form of the verb for Events.

Example: Luke 2:47

All who heard him were amazed at his *understanding* and his *answers.*

Understanding and *answers* are Events. And all who heard him were amazed because he understood and answered well.

1) Acts 8:32

as a sheep led to the *slaughter*

2) John 8:51

He will never see *death.*

3) Acts 16:26

Suddenly there was a great *earthquake*

4) Phil. 4:17

not that I seek a *gift*

5) Rom. 5:10

reconciled to God by the *death* of his Son

6) John 4:22

for *salvation* is *from* the Jews

7) 2 Cor. 9:15

Thanks be to God for his *inexpressible gift.*

8) 2 Thess. 1:11

Fulfill every good *resolve* and *work* of *faith* by his *power.*

9) Rom. 3:5
But if our *wickedness* serves to show the *justice* of God, what shall we say? That God is unjust to inflict *wrath* on us?

10) 2 Cor. 7:10
Godly *grief* produces a *repentance* that leads to *salvation* and brings no *regret*.

C. *Identifying the meaning components of a word.* "The experience or environment which a word symbolizes, regardless of how little or how much it refers to, is a unit of meaning. These units are divisible into parts called *semantic components*. Semantic components are the building blocks that are joined to give the meaning of a word; and they, as well as words, are divided into four different classes. These are also labeled Thing, Event, Abstraction and Relation" (Beekman-Callow, 1974, 67, 68).

In each of the following, what are the meaning components of the word in italics in the passage? Which is the nuclear component?

Example: Acts 27:16
And running under the lee of a small *island* called Clauda. . . .
The meaning components are *land, surrounded by,* and *water.*
Land is a Thing, *water* is a Thing, and *surrounded by* is a Relation.
The nuclear component is *land.*

1) Acts 7:36
He led them in the *wilderness* for forty years.

2) Acts 7:41
And they made a *calf* in those days, and offered a sacrifice.

3) Acts 7:44
Our fathers had the *tent* of witness in the wilderness.

4) Acts 8:13
seeing signs and great *miracles* performed

5) Acts 9:17
The Lord Jesus who *appeared* to you in the road . . . .

6) Acts 9:25
They let him down over the *wall.*

7) Acts 9:33
   He found a man who had been *bedridden* for eight years.

8) Acts 9:40
   But Peter knelt down and *prayed*.

9) Acts 9:43
   He stayed with Simon, a *tanner*.

10) Acts 10:42
    He commanded us to *preach* to the people.

D. *Identifying generic-specific changes.* Study the translation made for the word italicized in each of the following passages. Was the change from a) specific to generic, b) generic to specific, or c) one specific substituted for another specific?

Example: Matt. 6:28
   Consider the *lilies* of the field.
   Aguaruna: Think about the *flowers*.
      Answer: a

1) Acts 13:6
   They came upon a certain *magician* named Bar-Jesus.
   Aguaruna: There they saw a witchdoctor named Bar-Jesus who lived there.

2) John 10:12
   The *wolf* snatches them and scatters them.
   Aguaruna: The savage-animal grabbing at them causes them to scatter.

3) Acts 2:1
   They were all gathered in one place.
   Tenango Otomi: The believers were all gathered.

4) John 1:32
   and *it* remained on him
   Amuzgo: the Holy Spirit remained with him

5) Acts 1:10
   Two *men* stood by them in white robes.
   Aguaruna: Two people dressed in white clothes appeared by the side of those who stood looking.

6) Acts 2:29
   His *tomb* is with us to this day.
   Aguaruna: Even now one is able to see his burial place.

7) Acts 3:6
   I have no *silver* and *gold*.
   Isthmus Mixe: I don't have any money.

8) Acts 3:10
   and amazement at *what had happened* to him
   Huave: when they saw that the man with the crippled feet
   had been cured

E. *Using a more generic word.* What is a more generic word that
includes the specific word italicized in each of the following?

Example: 1 Thess. 2:7
   like a *nurse* taking care of her children
   A more generic word for *nurse* is *woman.*

1) Matt. 10:31
   You are of more value than many *sparrows.*

2) John 10:12
   He sees the *wolf* coming and leaves the sheep and *flees.*

3) 1 Peter 5:8
   like a roaring *lion*, seeking someone to devour

4) Rev. 14:16
   He swung his *sickle* on the earth.

5) Rev. 8:13
   I heard an *eagle* crying with a loud voice.

F. *Using a more specific word.* There are words and phrases in
Scripture that substitute for a previously stated referent. Certain
pro-verbs such as *do, happen, make,* and *act* may need to be
translated by the more specific action that they stand for. Rewrite the following, substituting the specific action referred to
instead of the word in italics.

Example: Acts 3:17
   I know that you *acted* in ignorance.
      Aguaruna: I know that you killed Jesus because you did
      not know that he was really the Son of God.

1) Mark 5:32
   He looked around to see who *had done* it.

2) Mark 11:28
   By what authority are you *doing these things?*

3) Luke 24:14
   talking with each other about *all these things that had happened*

4) John 8:40
   This is not what Abraham *did*. (Abraham *did* not *do this*.)

5) Acts 3:10
   They were filled with wonder and amazement at *what had happened* to him.

6) 1 Tim. 4:16
   By so doing you will save both yourself and your hearers.

G. *Identifying the pronominal referent.* Sometimes in the translation it is necessary to substitute the referent for a pronoun or other general nominal word. What is the referent of the italicized word in each of the following? Study the context carefully.

Example: Acts 13:25
   I am not *he*.
      Totonac: I am not the *Christ*.

1) Mark 16:19
   So then the Lord Jesus, after he had spoken to *them* . . . .

2) Luke 18:23
   But when he heard *this* he became sad.

3) John 2:16
   Take *these things* away.

4) Acts 5:11
   And great fear came upon all who heard *these things*.

5) Acts 7:7
   After *that* they shall come out and worship me.

6) Acts 27:44
   the *rest* on planks or on pieces of the ship

7) Rom. 11:7
   The elect obtained it, but the *rest* were hardened.

8) 1 Cor. 3:19
   "*He* catches the wise in their craftiness."

H. *Identifying the meaning components of some key words.* For each of the following sets of words, what is the generic component that they have in common that makes them members of the same semantic set? What is the generic class label for the set? What specifying components can you identify for each that make them contrast with the other words in the set?

Example: tabernacle, temple, synagogue
Generic components — shelter, used for religious purposes, used by the Jews
Generic class — kinds of shelters used for religious purposes by the Jews

Specifying components:

tabernacle	*temple*	*synagogue*
a) Place where God lived	a) Place where God lived	a) Place where people met for religious teaching
b) Temporary (movable)	b) Permanent	b) Permanent
c) Only one	c) Only one	c) Many in different places
d) People went to make sacrifices	d) People went to make sacrifices, pray, teach, learn, burn incense	d) People went for reading of the law, teaching, prayer

1) angel, demon, evil-spirit, Satan

2) prophet, angel, ~~messenger~~, apostle

3) disciple, apostle, believer

4) book, epistle, Scripture, Gospel

5) soldier, centurion, commander

6) repentance, conversion

7) Levite, priest, chief priest, scribe

CHAPTER 5

Analyzing Components of Meaning in a Word, Part 2

TEXT: Beekman-Callow, 1974, chapter 5

ADDITIONAL READING:

(See additional reading for chapter 4 of this manual)

SECTION 1. ANALYZING THE COMPONENTS OF MEANING OF WORDS

Use as many of the nine steps below (as outlined in the text [Beekman-Callow, chapter 5]) as are needed and analyze the components of meaning of the word indicated at the beginning of each drill. Use as context only the verses given, thus limiting your analysis to the meaning in these verses.

a) Listing the word in all its contexts.
b) Finding the generic class of the collocates.
c) Regrouping the contexts according to the collocates which belong to the same generic class.
d) Stating the generic class of each sense.
e) Stating the generic component by combining the generic term or expression of each sense with its collocational restriction.
f) Stating the generic class label for each sense.
g) Generating a semantic set for each sense.
h) Establishing the specifying components.
i) Checking to see that no extraneous members are included in the semantic set.

A. *Spirit*

1) Matt. 3:16
   And he saw the Spirit of God descending like a dove.

2) Matt. 4:1
   Then Jesus was led up by the Spirit into the wilderness.

45

3) Matt. 5:3
Blessed are the poor in spirit.

4) Matt. 12:43
When the unclean spirit has gone out of a man, he passes through waterless places seeking rest, but he finds none.

5) Matt. 26:41
The spirit indeed is willing, but the flesh is weak.

6) Mark 2:8
And immediately Jesus, perceiving in his spirit, said to them . . . .

7) Mark 6:49
When they saw him walking on the sea they thought it was a spirit. (KJV)

B. *Flesh*

1) Rom. 3:20
For no flesh will be justified in his sight by the works of the law. (KJV)

2) Rom. 8:3
For God has done what the law, weakened by the flesh, could not do: sending his own Son in the likeness of sinful flesh and for sin, he condemned sin in the flesh.

3) Rom. 8:13
If you live according to the flesh you will die.

4) Rom. 13:14
Make no provision for the flesh, to gratify its desires.

5) Rom. 14:21
It is good neither to eat flesh, nor drink wine. (KJV)

C. *Glory*

1) Matt. 4:8
The devil took him to a very high mountain, and showed him all the kingdoms of the world and the glory of them.

2) Matt. 6:2
Sound no trumpet before you as the hypocrites do in the synagogues and in the streets, that they may receive glory of men. (KJV)

3) Matt. 6:29
Solomon in all his glory was not arrayed like one of these.

4) Matt. 16:27
For the Son of man is to come with his angels in the glory of his Father.

5) Matt. 24:30
They will see the Son of man coming on the clouds of heaven with power and great glory.

6) Luke 2:9
The glory of the Lord shone around about them.

7) Luke 2:14
Glory to God in the highest.

8) Luke 2:32
a light for revelation to the Gentiles, and for glory to thy people Israel

9) John 1:14
We have beheld his glory, glory as of the only Son from the Father.

10) John 7:18
He who speaks on his own authority seeks his own glory, but he who seeks the glory of him who sent him is true.

SECTION 2. THE COMPONENTS OF MEANING OF PRONOUNS

ADDITIONAL READING:

Beekman, John, 1965, *NOT with Drills*, 124-176
Bishop, Eric F. F., 1953, "Pronominal Courtesy in the New Testament," *TBT*, 4/1, 32-34
Lofthouse, W. F., 1955, " 'I' and 'We' in the Pauline Letters," *TBT*, 6/2, 72-80
Nida, 1947, 265-67
Nida, 1964, 197
Nida and Taber, 1969, 112-13
Pickett, Velma B., 1964, "Those Problem Pronouns: *We, Us,* and *Our* in the New Testament," *TBT* 15/2, 88-92
Seely, Francis M., 1957, "Some Problems in Translating the Scriptures into Thai," *TBT* 8/2, 49-61
Swellengrebel, J. L., 1963, "Politeness and Translation in Balinese," *TBT* 14/4, 158-64

A. *Inclusive-exclusive.* "Many a Bible translator, working at the task of making the Scriptures speak a language of Asia, or the islands of the Pacific, or Africa, or Latin America finds himself faced with two different kinds of first person plural pronouns — one which includes the person spoken to (labelled by linguists 'inclusive') and the one which excludes the person spoken to (labelled by linguists 'exclusive')" (Pickett, 88).

> Example: In Luke 7:4, 5 the first "our" is inclusive, referring to the Jewish nation of which both the speakers and Jesus were a part. But the second "our" is no doubt exclusive, i.e., the synagogue in their town, of which Jesus was not a part (Pickett).

Would you use the inclusive or the exclusive "we" in the following passages for the italicized words? Make your decision on the basis of the context without reference to the articles which list the answers reached for certain languages, then check to see if you agree with the Zapotec, Mazatec, etc.

1) Titus 1:3
   with which *I* have been entrusted by command of God our Savior

2) Titus 3:5
   not because of deeds done by *us* in righteousness

3) 1 Thess. 1:3
   remembering before *our* God and Father your work of faith

4) Acts 2:8
   How is it that *we* hear each of *us* in his own native language?

5) 1 John 2:1
   we have an advocate with the Father, Jesus Christ

6) Luke 11:4
   forgive *us* *our* sins, for we ourselves forgive everyone who is indebted to *us*

7) Acts 2:32
   This Jesus God raised up, and of that *we* all are witnesses.

8) Luke 24:20
   and how *our* chief priests and rulers delivered him up to be condemned to death, and crucified him

9) Luke 9:49
   John answered, "Master, *we* saw a man casting out demons in your name."
10) John 18:31
   It is not lawful for *us* to put any man to death.

B. *Number.* In Pame, as well as in many other languages, there are pronominal endings to indicate dual number and different pronominal endings to indicate plural of more than two. In Pame, Acts 5:8 — "Tell me whether *you* sold the land for so much" — the translation must use the dual second-person pronoun to indicate *you*, since Peter, when speaking to Sapphira, was talking about Ananias and Sapphira.

Assume you are translating into a language that has the following pronouns and rewrite the passages indicated, using these pronouns rather than the English pronouns.

na — I	tu — you	no — he
ji — we (2)	si — you (2)	ra — they (2)
ro — we (plural)	ma — you (plural)	so — they (plural)

You may need to supply some extra pronouns. Check your Bible for context. Assume that the same form is used for subjective, objective, and possessive pronouns, i.e., *no* means "he," "him," and "his," *ji* means "we," "us," and "ours," etc. (In actual translation you would be making other adjustments also, and in the structure of the receptor language not all pronouns would necessarily be retained.)

Example: Acts 3:5
   And he fixed his attention upon them, expecting to receive something from them.
   And *no* fixed *no* attention upon *ra*, expecting to receive something from *ra*.

1) Acts 3:4
   And Peter directed *his* gaze at *him*, with John, and said, "Look at *us*."
2) Acts 6:3
   Therefore, brethren, pick out from among *you* seven men whom *we* may appoint to this duty.
3) Acts 7:26
   He appeared to *them* as *they* were quarreling and would have reconciled *them*, saying, "men, *you* are brethren."

4) Acts 8:15
. . . who came down and prayed for *them*, that *they* might receive the Holy Spirit.

5) Acts 8:17
Then *they* laid *their* hands on *them*, and *they* received the Holy Spirit.

6) Acts 8:39
When *they* came up out of the water, the Spirit caught up Philip; and the eunuch saw *him* no more.

7) Acts 9:39
So Peter rose and went with *them*. And when *he* had come, *they* took *him* to the upper room.

8) Acts 11:26
When *he* had found *him*, *he* brought *him* to Antioch. For a whole year *they* met with the church.

9) Acts 13:2, 3
"Set apart for me Barnabas and Saul for the work to which *I* have called *them*." Then after fasting and praying *they* laid *their* hands on *them* and sent *them* off.

10) Acts 16:35-37
And the jailer reported the words to Paul, saying, "The magistrates have sent to let *you* go, now, therefore come out and go in peace." But Paul said to *them*, "*They* have beaten *us* publicly, uncondemned, men who are Roman citizens, and have thrown *us* into prison; and do *they* now cast *us* out secretly? . . ."

C. *Honorifics.* In Greek and in European languages such as Dutch and English the third person pronoun does not present much difficulty. In Balinese the situation becomes more complicated, for one has at least four pronouns for the third person: to indicate a very important person (*ida*), an important person (*dané*), a person of lower standing spoken of in a polite manner (*ipun*), and such a person spoken of in a familiar manner (*ia*). *Dané*, the pronoun of the slightly less important person of the third caste, is also in use for people of lower caste who through their official position, age, or ability have a right to be respected, and for those with whom one is trying to ingratiate oneself (Swellengrebel, p. 160).

Example: In the gospel stories these simple artisans and fishermen were not of such high standing. So here *ia* and *ipun* are used. In the Acts, however, the position of apostles such as Peter and John is expressed by the use of the word *dané*.

Assume you are translating into a language such as Balinese. Which of the four pronouns might you choose in the following passages? (It is impossible to know for sure without being familiar with the culture of the Balinese, so your choice will probably not equal that of a Balinese speaker, but try to decide on the basis of the position the person mentioned had in Jewish culture and the respect that those writing about them might have included.)

> *ida* — very important
> *dané* — important
> *ipun* — low standing but polite manner
> *ia* — low standing but familiar manner

Substitute one of these for the italicized words in the following:

1) Matt. 2:7, 8
   Then Herod summoned the wise men secretly and *he* sent them to Bethlehem.

2) Matt. 2:14
   And *he* rose and took the child and *his* mother by night, and departed to Egypt.

3) Mark 1:42
   And immediately the leprosy left *him*, and *he* was made clean.

4) Mark 3:1-5
   Again *he* entered the synagogue, and a man was there who had a withered hand. And *he* said to the man, "Stretch out your hand." *He* stretched it out.

5) Mark 12:1, 2
   A man planted a vineyard, and *he* sent a servant to the tenants.

6) Mark 14:11
   And *he* sought an opportunity to betray *him*.

7) Mark 16:9, 10
   He appeared first to Mary Magdalene, from whom *he* had cast seven demons. *She* went and . . . .

8) Luke 4:10
   For it is written, '*He* will give *his* angels charge of you . . . .'

9) John 19:6
   When the chief priests and the officers saw *him*, they cried out, "Crucify *him*, crucify *him!*" Pilate said to them, "Take *him* yourselves and crucify *him*, for I find no crime in *him*."

10) Acts 9:19, 20
    For several days *he* was with the disciples at Damascus. And in the synagogues . . . *he* proclaimed Jesus, saying, "*He* is the Son of God."

SECTION 3. THE COMPONENTS OF MEANING IN KINSHIP TERMS

ADDITIONAL READING:

Doke, C. M., 1958, "Some Difficulties in Bible Translation into a Bantu Language," *TBT* 9/2, 57, 58

Nida, 1947, 180-82

Nida, 1964, 82-87

Seely, Francis M., 1957, "Some Problems in Translating the Scriptures into Thai," *TBT* 8/2, 54

"In Piro one must not translate literally the word 'son' in Mark 2:5. The Piros do not speak in this manner to those who are not specifically their own children; and to do this would be implying that this was Jesus' own son, who was let down through the roof. The implications of Jesus' neglect of his own son, with the obvious inference that he was married, would, of course, make a literal translation entirely wrong. However, in a similar circumstance a Piro would say 'young man,' even though the age might differ considerably. This use of 'young man' is, of course, necessary and entirely legitimate" (Nida, Eugene A., 1950, "Translation or Paraphrase," *TBT*, 1/3, 105).

A. *Son.* In a language in which *son* means only "the actual male child of a man" and is not used in any general (extended) way, how might you translate the following?

Example: Mark 3:17
   sons of thunder
      those who are like thunder

1) Ps. 77:15
   thy people, the sons of Jacob and Joseph

2) Matt. 1:20
Joseph, son of David

3) Acts 4:36
Son of encouragement

4) Eph. 3:5
which was not made known to the sons of men in other generations

5) 1 Tim. 1:18
This charge I commit to you, Timothy, my son . . . .

B. *Daughter.* In the same language *daughter* means only "the actual female child of a man." How might you try translating the following?

1) Matt. 9:22
He said, "Take heart, daughter . . . ."

2) Mark 5:34
Daughter, your faith has made you well . . . .

3) Luke 13:16
this woman, a daughter of Abraham

4) Luke 23:28
Daughters of Jerusalem, do not weep for me . . . .

5) John 12:15
Fear not, daughter of Zion . . . .

C. *Brother.* Assume you are translating into a language in which *brother* is not used in an extended, general way. How might you try translating the following?

1) Acts 9:17
So Ananias said, "Brother Saul . . . ."

2) Rom. 14:10
Why do you pass judgment on your brother?

3) Rom. 14:15
If your brother is being injured by what you eat . . . .

4) 1 Cor. 16:12
As for our brother Apollos . . . .

5) James 4:11
He that speaks evil against a brother or judges his brother . . . .

D. *Older brother and younger brother.* "(In Thai) one cannot say simply 'brother.' There are only two words to choose from. One means *older brother* and the other means *younger brother*" (Seely, 1957, 54).

Assuming you are translating into one of the many languages that make this distinction between older and younger brother, which do you think you might use in the following passages?

Example: John 1:41
He first found his brother Simon . . . .
Agta: He first found his *younger brother*, Simon . . . .

1) Matt. 4:18
He saw two brothers (translate men), Simon who is called Peter and Andrew his *brother*.

2) Matt. 10:2
The names of the twelve apostles . . . James the son of Zebedee, and John his *brother* . . . .

3) Matt. 22:24
If a man dies his *brother* must marry the widow . . . .

4) Mark 6:17
For Herod had sent and seized John for the sake of Herodias, his *brother* Philip's wife.

5) Luke 12:13
One of the multitude said to him, "Teacher, bid my *brother* divide the inheritance with me."

6) Luke 15:32
It was fitting to make merry and be glad, for this your *brother* was dead, and is alive.

E. *An example from Aguaruna.* In Aguaruna there are three words for the two English words "brother" and "sister." How they are used can best be seen by the following chart. A man's brother is *yatsug*; his sister *ubag*; a woman's brother is *ubag*; her sister *kaig*.

	of male	of female
male sibling	*yatsug*	*ubag*
female sibling	*ubag*	*kaig*

Which of these three words would you use to translate the following passages:

Example: Mark 6:3
Is not this the *brother* of James and Joses
. . . and are not his *sisters* with us?
brother — yatsug
sister — ubag

1) Gen. 20:2
And Abraham said of Sarah his wife, "She is my *sister*."

2) Matt. 4:18
Andrew his *brother*

3) Mark 3:35
Whoever does the will of God is my *brother*, and *sister* . . . .

4) Luke 10:39
She had a *sister* called Mary.

5) John 11:1
the village of Mary and her *sister* Martha

6) John 11:2
It was Mary whose *brother* Lazarus was ill.

7) John 11:23
Jesus said unto her, "Your *brother* will rise again."

8) John 11:39
the *sister* of the dead man

F. *Siblings.* Do the same passages again, using the following kinship system with only two words for siblings, one for male and female sibling of male, another for male and female sibling of female.

sibling of male — *nami*
sibling of female — *rumo*

SECTION 4. OBLIGATORY POSSESSION

ADDITIONAL READING:

Nida, 1964, 205-6

Thompson, William E., 1950, "Gender, Pronominal Reference, and Possession in Guajiro," *TBT* 1/4, 166-69

"Certain terms in Guajiro are regularly possessed. For example, one rarely hears 'father' or 'son' without some possessive prefix to indicate whose father or son is being talked about. One can by persevering elicit a form such as 'son' without any explicit indication of possession, but the form is unnatural and in some contexts means 'an indefinite person's son,' i.e., 'somebody's son.'

"The parts of the body also occur with possessive prefixes. One does not normally speak of 'eye,' 'arm,' or 'leg' but rather of 'his eye,' 'her arm,' or 'the man's leg.' Hence in translating 'eye for an eye and tooth for a tooth' one must say 'one person's eye for another person's eye and one person's tooth for another person's tooth.'

"As noted above, there are certain types of nouns which are obligatorily possessed. A few additional illustrations of this feature of Guajiro may make the picture clearer. For example, in John 3:35 it is necessary to say, 'The Father loves his Son.' Otherwise the meaning would be that the Father loved 'somebody's son,' but not his own. Similarly, in John 5:19-21 the context requires us to substitute 'his Father' for certain occurrences of 'the Father' and 'his Son' for certain occurrences of 'the Son.'

"In John 14:9-11 there is a somewhat different type of problem, for in this section Jesus speaks of himself in the first person. Accordingly, 'the Father' becomes 'my father'; in verse 9 one must translate, 'He who has seen me has seen my Father'" (Thompson, 1950, 166, 169).

Assuming that you are translating into a language like Guajiro described above, rewrite each of the following phrases, adding either a possessive pronoun or a noun to indicate the possessor of all *body parts* and all *kinship terms* (father, son, child, etc.).

Example: Rev. 1:7
Every *eye* will see him.
All people will see him with their eyes.

A. *Examples based on Guajiro.*

1) Matt. 10:28
Do not fear those who kill the *body.*

2) Luke 1:59
They came to circumcise the *child.*

3) Luke 15:13
The younger *son* gathered all he had.

4) John 14:13
that the Father may be glorified in the *Son*

5) Gal. 4:2
until the date set by the *father*

6) Gal. 4:6
because you are *sons*, God has sent

7) Heb. 10:5
but a *body* hast thou prepared for me

8) James 2:16
things needed for the *body*

9) James 3:10
From the same *mouth* come blessing and cursing.

10) Rev. 4:6
four living creatures, full of *eyes* in front and behind

B. *Examples based on Guajiro, continued.*

1) Matt. 6:22 .
The *eye* is the lamp of the *body*.

2) Matt. 6:25
and the *body* more than clothing?

3) Matt. 10:37
he who loves *son* or *daughter* more than me

4) Matt. 11:27
No one knows the *Son* except the *Father*.

5) Matt. 27:59
Joseph took the *body*.

6) Mark 8:18
Having *eyes* do you not see, and having *ears* do you not hear?

7) Luke 1:13
Elizabeth will bear you a *son*.

8) Luke 1:80
The *child* grew and became strong.

9) 2 Cor. 4:10
always carrying in the *body*

10) 1 John 2:22
he who denies the *Father* and the *Son*

C. *Obligatory possession and kinship terms.* Rewrite John 14:8-14, indicating the possessor of all kinship terms.

D. *Obligatory possession and body parts.* Rewrite 1 Corinthians 12:12-27, indicating the possessor of all body parts mentioned, including the word *body.*

E. *Obligatory possession, number, and inclusive-exclusive.* In the following exercise the word requiring a possessive pronoun is italicized. Select from the list of pronouns the one you would use to modify each italicized word.

na — my	tu — your	no — his, hers
ju — our (2 incl.)	si — your (2)	ra — theirs (2)
pu — our (2 excl.)		
ro — our (pl. incl.)	ma — your (pl.)	so — their (pl.)
ki — our (pl. excl.)		

Example: Acts 1:7
It is not for you to know the times or seasons which the *Father* has fixed . . . .
ro — our (pl. incl.)

1) Luke 9:49
John answered, "*Master,* we saw a man casting out demons . . . ."

2) Luke 15:31
And he said to him, "*Son* you are always with me . . . ."

3) Gal. 1:1
and God the *Father,* who raised him from the dead

4) Rom. 2:29
real circumcision is a matter of the *heart*

5) John 1:38
And they said to him, "*Rabbi* . . . where are you staying?"

6) Luke 1:59
They came to circumcise the *child.*

7) John 6:25
They said to him, "*Rabbi,* when did you come here?"

8) Matt. 10:28

And do not fear those who kill the *body* but cannot kill the *soul*.

SECTION 5. THE COMPONENTS OF MEANING IN TENSE AND ASPECT MARKERS

ADDITIONAL READING:

Nida, 1947, 250-63
Nida, 1964, 196-206
Nida and Taber, 1969, 113-18
Vielhauer, Adolf, 1956, "A Glimpse into the Workshop of a Bible Translator," *TBT* 7/3, 122-123

A. *Tense.* Vielhauer, in describing problems of translation into Bali, says, "Moreover the past and future in the Bali tongue are divided into three grades. The first grade signifies the past or future respectively immediately connected with the present. The second grade is separated from the present by a certain period of time, but the action happening on the same day. The third grade is separated from the present by at least one night" (Vielhauer, 1956, 123).

Assuming you are translating into Bali, which of the following seven tenses would you choose for each of the verbs italicized in the exercise? Check the context for the time sequence. In narration, the point of reference is the time when the Bible book was written, but in direct quotes it may be found by studying the context.

Present: right now
Past 1: present but completed, immediate past
Past 2: recent past, within the same day
Past 3: further past, earlier than the same day
Future 1: present but not yet complete
Future 2: near future, within the same day
Future 3: more distant future, later than same day

Example: Acts 5:3

But Peter *said*, "Ananias, why *has* Satan *filled* your heart to lie to the Holy Spirit and to keep back part of the proceeds of the land?"

said — past 3, because it was said long before Luke recorded it
has filled — past 2

1) Acts 1:11
   This Jesus, who *was taken up* from you into heaven, *will come* in the same way . . . .

2) John 10:25
   Jesus *answered* them, "I *told* you, and you *do not* believe."

3) John 18:26
   One of the servants asked, "Did I not *see* you in the garden with him?"

4) John 18:38
   He *told* them, "I *find* no crime in him."

5) John 19:15
   Pilate *said* to them, "S*hall* I *crucify* your King?"

6) John 20:15
   (Mary) *said* to him, "Sir, if you *have carried* him away, tell me where you *laid* him."

7) John 20:25
   So the other disciple *told* him (Thomas), "We *have seen* the Lord." But he *said* unto them, "Unless I *see* in his hands the print . . . ."

8) Mark 10:32-34
   And taking the twelve again, he *began to tell* them what *was to happen* to him, saying, "Behold, we *are going* up to Jerusalem; and the Son of man *will be delivered* to the chief priests . . . and after three days he *will rise*."

B. *Aspect.* Vielhauer, in describing Bali, indicates a further problem in the aspects of the verbs. He says, "Moreover you always have to consider whether an action is thought of as only once happening or as a continued or an often repeated action, because the Bali has different tenses for the once occurring and for the repeated action of a verb" (Vielhauer, 1956, 123). Which of the three tense-aspects would you choose for the italicized words?

   a) unit action (happened once)
   b) repeated action (happened several times in sequence)
   c) continued action (one action but extended over a period of time)

Example: Mark 1:39
And he went throughout all Galilee, *preaching* in their synagogues and *casting out* demons.
Repeated action (Jesus preached in various synagogues and cast out demons several times.)

1) Mark 1:40, 41
And a leper *came* to him *beseeching* him . . . moved with pity, he *stretched* out his hand and *touched* him.

2) Mark 2:1
It *was reported* that he *was* at home.

3) Mark 2:3
bringing to him a paralytic *carried* by four men

4) Mark 2:17
And when Jesus *heard* it, he *said* to them . . . .

5) Mark 2:18
Now John's disciples and the Pharisees *were fasting*.

6) Mark 3:13, 14
And he *went up* into the hills, and *called to* him those whom he *desired*; and they *came* to him. And he *appointed* twelve.

7) Mark 4:2
And he *taught* them many things in parables, and in his teachings he *said* to them

8) Mark 4:37, 38
And a great storm *arose*, and the waves *beat* into the boat, but he was in the stern, *asleep* on the cushion; and they *woke* him.

9) Mark 5:27
She had *heard* the reports about Jesus, and *came up* behind him in the crowd and *touched* his garment.

10) Mark 5:36
But *ignoring* what they said, Jesus *said* to the ruler

C. *"Dead" suffix in Amuesha.* In a number of languages, including Amuesha of Peru, there is an obligatory morpheme that must be suffixed to the name of any person referred to after his death.

An interesting problem arises in the transfiguration account as to whether or not Moses' name should have the "dead" suffix. The translators have decided to leave the suffix off the name of Moses in the transfiguration story, since his obvious physical presence would be contradictory to the reference to his death. They are using it with the names of the characters of the Old Testament when they are mentioned in the New in other contexts and with the names of characters of the New Testament only if they have reason to believe that the person was dead *when the record was written.*

Following their way of handling this problem, on which of the following italicized names would you put the "dead" suffix?

1) Matt. 2:7
   Then *Herod* summoned the wise men secretly.

2) Acts 1:5
   for *John* baptized with water

3) Acts 1:16
   concerning *Judas* who was guide to those who arrested *Jesus*

4) Acts 5:1
   a man named *Ananias* with his wife *Sapphira* sold

5) Acts 7:1, 2
   And the *high priest* said, "Is this so?" and *Stephen* said . . .

6) Acts 8:1
   And *Saul* was consenting to his death.

7) Acts 8:9
   There was a man named *Simon.*

8) Acts 9:36
   Now there was at Joppa a disciple named *Tabitha,* which means Dorcas or Gazelle. She was full of good works.

9) Acts 12:1, 2
   About that time *Herod* the king laid violent hand upon some who belonged to the church. He killed *James* the brother of *John* with the sword.

10) 1 Cor. 16:19
    The churches of Asia send greetings. *Aquila* and *Prisca* send greetings.

CHAPTER 6

The Nature of Multiple Senses

TEXT: Beekman-Callow, 1974, chapter 6

ADDITIONAL READING:

Aulie, Wilbur, 1957, "Figures of Speech in the Chol New Testament," *TBT* 8/3, 109-13

Beekman, John, 1967, "Metonymy and Synecdoche," *NOT* 23: 12-25

Callow, John, 1973, "Two Approaches to the Analysis of Meaning," *NOT* 48: 23-27

Elkins, Richard, 1973, "The Structure of Some Semantic Sets of W. B. Manobo," *NOT* 41:10-21

Nida, 1964, 30-58, 93-119

Nida and Taber, 1969, 56-98

A. *Various Senses.* "A single word may have various senses. These senses may be classified as primary, secondary, and figurative. The primary sense is the first meaning or usage which a word apart from context will suggest to most people. Secondary senses are those which the same word carries and which are related to one another and to the primary meaning by sharing some thread of meaning. Figurative senses are based on associative relations to the primary sense" (Beekman-Callow, 1974, 94).

In each of the following sets of verses, the same word is used but in only one verse is it used in its primary sense. In the others it is used in a secondary sense or a figurative sense. Identify the usages as primary, secondary, or figurative.

Example: a) Luke 16:24
Send Lazarus to dip the tip of his finger in water, and cool my *tongue.*
b) 1 Peter 3:10
Let him keep his *tongue* from evil.

a) primary   b) figurative

1) a) Matt. 8:8
   Lord, I am not worthy to have you under my *roof*.
   b) Mark 2:4
   And when they could not get near him because of the crowd, they removed the *roof* above him.
   c) Ezek. 3:26
   I will make your tongue cleave to the *roof* of your mouth.

2) a) Matt. 15:11
   Not what goes into the *mouth* defiles a man.
   b) Luke 19:22
   I will condemn you out of your own *mouth*, you wicked servant!
   c) Gen. 42:27
   He saw his money in the *mouth* of his sack.

3) a) John 15:18
   If the *world* hates you, know that it has hated me before it hated you.
   b) Matt. 13:35
   I will utter what has been hidden since the foundation of the *world*.
   c) 1 John 5:4
   This is the victory that overcometh the *world*, our faith.

4) a) Mark 9:42
   It would better for him if a great millstone were hung around his *neck* and he were thrown into the sea.
   b) Rom. 16:4
   who risked their *necks* for my life

5) a) 2 Tim. 4:17
   So I was rescued from the lion's *mouth*.
   b) Rev. 1:16
   From his *mouth* issued a sharp two-edged sword.
   c) Gen. 29:2
   The stone on the well's *mouth* was large.

B. *Figurative senses, based on contiguity.* In each of the following, the word italicized is being used in a figurative sense based on contiguity. Rewrite the passage using nonfigurative wording.

Example: 2 Pet. 3:12
Waiting for and hastening the coming of the *day* of God.
Waiting for and hastening the coming of the day when God will judge ungodly men.

1) Luke 22:14
And when the *hour* came, he sat at table.

2) Matt. 3:5
Then went out to him *Jerusalem* and all *Judea*.

3) Luke 1:32
The Lord God will give to him the *throne* of his father David.

4) John 15:18
If the *world* hates you, know that it has hated me . . . .

5) Matt. 5:13
You are the salt of the *earth*.

6) Mark 3:25
And if a *house* is divided against itself, that *house* will not be able to stand.

C. *Figurative senses, based on part-whole associations.* In each of the following, the word italicized is being used in a figurative sense based on part-whole association. Rewrite the passage, using nonfigurative wording.

Example: Matt. 8:8
Lord, I am not worthy to have you come under my *roof*.
Lord, I am not worthy to have you come into my house.

1) Luke 12:19
I will say to my *soul*

2) Eph. 6:22
I have sent him that he may encourage your *hearts*.

3) John 1:19
When the *Jews* sent priests and Levites from Jerusalem to ask him

4) Matt. 27:4
I have sinned in betraying innocent *blood*.

5) Luke 7:27
Behold, I send my messenger before thy *face.*

6) Rom. 12:1
Present your *bodies* as a living sacrifice.

7) James 1:26
If any one does not bridle his tongue but deceives his *heart,*
this man's religion is vain.

8) Rev. 10:4
I heard a *voice* from heaven saying

D. *Meaning in Context.* The senses intended by secondary and
figurative senses are determined by the context in which the word
or phrase is used. State the contextual meaning of the italicized
word and what in the context determines the meaning which you
assign to the word or phrase in this passage.

Example: Titus 3:13
Do your best to speed Zenas and Apollos on their way; *see*
that they lack nothing.
See is used in the sense of *take care (look after).*
This meaning is indicated by the context of someone going
on a journey and the word *lack.*

1) Mark 7:2, 3
They saw that some of his disciples ate with hands defiled,
that is *unwashed.* (For the Pharisees, and all the Jews, do
not eat unless they wash their hands, observing the tradition
of the elders . . . .)

2) Luke 1:53
He has *filled* the hungry with good things.

3) Acts 5:3
Why has Satan *filled* your heart to lie to the Holy Spirit
and to keep back part of the proceeds.

4) Acts 13:22
And when he had removed him, he *raised up* David to be
their king.

5) Acts 13:11, 12
Immediately mist and *darkness fell* upon him and he went
about seeking people to lead him by the hand. Then the
proconsul believed, when he saw what had occurred . . . .

CHAPTER 7

Translating Multiple Senses

TEXT: Beekman-Callow, 1974, chapter 7

ADDITIONAL READING:

Beekman, John, 1967, "Metonymy and Synecdoche," *NOT* 23: 12-15

Beekman, John, 1965, "Ambiguity or Obscurity of Pronominal Reference," *NOT* 16:7-12

Beekman, John, 1965, "Obligatory Inclusion of First and/or Second Person," *NOT* 16:6-7

Beekman, John, 1965, "Extended Usage of Number and Person," *NOT* 19

Beekman, John, ed., 1965, *NOT with Drills*, Summer Institute of Linguistics, 124-76

Butler, Inez M., 1965, "Implicit Exclusiveness in Villa Alta Zapotec," *NOT* 16:4-5

Lithgow, David R., 1970, "Impersonal Pronouns in Some Melanesian Languages of New Guinea," *TBT* 21/3, 137

Meader, Robert, 1966, "Spirit in the New Testament," *NOT* 20:18-21

Moore, Bruce R., 1973, "Symbolic Action and Synecdoche," *NOT* 49:14-15

Nida, Eugene A., 1955, "Problems in Translating Scripture into Shilluk, Anuak and Nuer," *TBT* 6/2, 55-63

de Waard, Jon, 1971, "Do you use 'clean language'?" (Old Testament Euphemisms and Their Translation), *TBT* 22/3, 107-15

VanDeWater, Clinton, 1973, "An Exegetical Examination of New Testament Usage of *Katharos*, 'Clean,'" *NOT* 49:21-26

Section 1. Extended Use of Pronouns

A. *Extended use of plural for singular.* "Some first person plural forms in the New Testament refer to one specific first person. This extended use of the first person plural is commonly known as the editorial we . . . for example, in 1 John 1:4 the phrase "we write" cannot in many languages apply equally to others besides the author unless joint authorship in the fullest sense of the term is assumed" (Beekman, 1965, *NOT* 19:1, 2).

Study each of the following in its context to determine whether the plural person is being used in an extended usage and refers to a singular person or whether it is being used in a literal sense in reference to more than one person. Answer by writing either "extended" or "literal."

1) Matt. 9:14

   Then the disciples of John came to him, saying, "Why do *we* and the Pharisees fast?"

2) Heb. 2:5

   For it was not to angels that God subjected the world to come, of which *we* are speaking.

3) Heb. 5:11

   About this *we* have much to say.

4) Acts 20:7

   On the first day of the week, when *we* were gathered together

5) 2 Cor. 10:11

   Let such people understand that what *we* say by letter when absent, *we* do when present.

6) 2 Cor. 8:1

   We want you to know, brethren, about the grace of God which has been shown

7) Acts 24:4

   But I beg you in your kindness to hear *us* briefly.

8) John 16:30

   Now *we* know that you know all things.

9) Heb. 8:1
Now the point in what *we* are saying is this: *we* have such a high priest.

10) Heb. 9:5
Of these things *we* cannot now speak in detail.

B. *Extended use of singular for plural.* "In some languages, a first person statement . . . is easily appropriated as personal, as for example, 'I can do all things through Christ.' . . . Unfortunately for some translators, this is not the case in the language in which they are translating. What is said in the first person singular immediately suggests in most contexts, that it is not true of those addressed" (Beekman, 1965, *NOT* 19:3).

For example, in Aguacateco of Guatemala the *I* had to be changed to *we* to avoid this problem in 1 Corinthians 13:12: "Now I know in part; then I shall understand fully, even as I have been fully understood."

In some languages general statements that are in the singular must be changed to plural if they are to have universal application. Study each of the following in context to discover whether the singular person is being used in an extended usage and applies in a general way or whether it is being used in a literal sense and applies to Paul only. Answer by writing "general" or "Paul only."

1) 1 Cor. 13:1
If *I* speak in the tongues of men and angels, but have not love

2) 1 Cor. 14:6
Now, brethren, if *I* come to you speaking in tongues, how shall I benefit you?

3) 1 Cor. 10:29
For why should *my* liberty be determined by another man's scruples?

4) 1 Cor. 11:23
For I received from the Lord what *I* also delivered to you, that the Lord Jesus

5) 1 Cor. 7:16
Wife, how do *you* know whether *you* will save *your* husband?

C. *Extended use of person.* In some passages the third-person noun or pronoun is used when one is referring to himself and so the referent is really first person. Jesus said, "No one has ascended into heaven but *he* who descended from heaven, the Son of Man" (John 3:13). The pronoun *he* refers to Jesus himself. In some languages the first-person pronoun would have to be used in the translation. In some instances third person is also used in referring to a real second person. In 1 Timothy 1:2, Paul begins his letter by writing, "To Timothy . . . ." Since Timothy is the person being addressed, it may need to be translated with a second person by saying, "To you, Timothy . . . ." In each of the following, determine to whom the italicized word actually refers and rewrite the passage, making a change of person so that the person is indicated by a literal rather than extended use of the pronoun. Study the context for help.

   Examples: John 5:26
     For as the Father has life in himself, so he has granted the *Son* also to have life in himself.
      As the Father has life in himself, so he has granted to me, his Son, also to have life in myself.
     John 1:51 You will see heaven opened, and the angels of God ascending and descending upon the Son of Man.
      Aguaruna: You will see God open the door of heaven and those sent from God descending and ascending at the place where I am, the one who was born becoming man.

  1) John 5:28
    For the hour is coming when all who are in the tombs will hear *his* voice.

  2) Rev. 2:1
    The words of him who holds the seven stars in *his* right hand

  3) John 20:4
    But the *other disciple* outran Peter and reached the tomb first.

  4) Rom. 1:7
    To *all* God's beloved in Rome, who are called to be saints.

  5) Jude 1
    To *those* who are called, beloved in God.

6) John 10:36
Do you say of *him* whom the Father consecrated and sent . . . ?

7) John 17:2
Since thou hast given *him* power over all flesh.

8) John 20:10
Then the *disciples* went back to *their* homes.

9) Luke 1:45
And blessed is *she* who believed that there would be a fulfillment.

10) 3 John 1
The *elder* to the beloved *Gaius*, whom I love in truth.

D. *Implicit exclusiveness.* In Villa Alta Zapotec the use of the second- and third-person pronouns excludes the first person. For example, a literal translation of "they are justified by his grace" (Rom. 3:24) would exclude the writer and so the translation must read "we are justified . . . ." In John 3:22, the clause "After this Jesus and his disciples went" would have to be translated, "After this, Jesus and we disciples went" in order to include John as one of the disciples. Colossians 3:1, "If then you have been raised with Christ, seek the things that are above," would need to be translated with first person: "Since we have been raised with Christ, we should seek those things that are above."

Rewrite each of the following so that the speaker (writer) is not excluded.

1) 1 Cor. 6:11
You were washed, you were sanctified, you were justified in the name of the Lord Jesus Christ.

2) Rom. 6:17
You who were once slaves of sin have become obedient.

3) Rom. 1:16
It is the power of God for salvation to the Jew first and also to the Greek.

4) Matt. 10:1
And he called to him his twelve disciples and gave them authority

5) John 6:3
He sat down there with his disciples.

6) Rom. 6:20
When you were slaves of sin, you were free in regard to righteousness.

7) John 4:9
For Jews have no dealings with Samaritans.

8) Col. 2:20
If with Christ you died to the elemental spirits of the universe, why do you live as if you still belonged to the world?

9) Eph. 2:1
And you he made alive, when you were dead through the trespasses and sins

10) 1 Cor. 3:16
Do you not know that you are God's temple and that God's Spirit dwells in you?

E. *Review.* Identify the usage of the italicized pronoun in each of the following passages by labeling it a, b, c, or d, according to the following designations:

a) extended use of plural for singular
b) extended use of singular for plural
c) extended use of person
d) not an extended use

Review the introductions of Sections A, B, and C before you begin.

1) John 3:14, 15
And as Moses lifted up the serpent in the wilderness, so must the Son of man be lifted up, that whoever believes in *him* may have eternal life.

2) 2 Cor. 1:13
For *we* write you nothing but what you can read and understand.

3) 2 Cor. 1:5
   For as *we* share abundantly in Christ's sufferings, so through Christ we share abundantly in comfort too.

4) John 9:37
   Jesus said to him, "You have seen him, and it is *he* who speaks to you."

5) 2 Thess. 1:3
   We are bound to give thanks to God always for you.

6) John 10:36
   Do you say of *him* whom the Father consecrated and sent into the world, 'You are blaspheming,' because I said . . .

7) John 9:27
   He answered them, "*I* have told you already, and you would not listen."

8) 1 Cor. 13:2
   And if *I* have prophetic powers, and understand all mysteries, but have not love, I am nothing.

F. *General pronouns.* "Where English employs *everyone, each, whoever,* and *any* the Shilluk, Anuak, and Nuer use plural number. Instead of English *whosoever,* one must say *all who.* 'Love thy neighbour as thyself' must be translated as 'Love your neighbours as yourselves' if the admonition is to apply to all and if one is to love more than just one neighbor" (Nida, 1955, 58).

Rewrite the following, changing the generic word or words to plural and adjusting other words affected by the change.

1) Eph. 4:32
   Be kind to *one another.*

2) John 3:16
   Whoever believes in him should not perish.

3) Acts 2:3
   And there appeared to them tongues as of fire, distributed and resting on *each one* of them.

4) Luke 6:30
Give to *every one* who begs from you.

5) Rom. 13:10
Love does no wrong to *a neighbor*.

G. *Review.* In the following, make the same adjustment as in F above and, in addition, change all abstract nouns to verb phrases. You may need to change negatives to positives.

Example: 1 John 2:15
If *any one* loves the world, love for the Father is not in him.
All who love the world do not truly love the Father.

1) 1 John 3:4
Every one who commits sin is guilty of lawlessness.

2) John 6:35
I am the bread of life; *he* who comes to me shall not hunger.

3) John 6:37
Him who comes to me I will not cast out.

4) 1 John 4:8
He who does not love does not know God; for God is love.

5) 1 Cor. 3:8
He who plants and *he* who waters are equal, and *each* shall receive *his* wages according to *his* labor.

6) John 12:25
He who loves *his* life loses it, and *he* who hates *his* life in this world will keep it for eternal life.

7) John 12:47
If *any one* hears my sayings and does not keep them . . . ?

8) John 14:23
If a *man* loves me, *he* will keep my word.

SECTION 2. FIGURATIVE SENSES AND SYMBOLIC ACTIONS

A. *Metonymy* is the substitution of one term for another having an associative relationship with it. In some languages, e.g., Huix-teco of Mexico, this figure of speech is not used and so the translation must restate what is meant without using the substitution. Give the meaning of the italicized metonymies and tell what the associative relationship is between the two.

Example: Phil. 1:6
  the day of Jesus Christ
    "day" stands for the event of the "coming" — time is substituted for the event that will happen at that time.

1) Matt. 7:22
   On that day many will say to me, "Lord, Lord . . . ."

2) Mark 4:29
   He puts in the *sickle.*

3) Luke 1:32
   He will give him the *throne* of his father David.

4) John 17:14
   The *world* has hated them because they are not of the *world.*

5) Acts 5:28
   to bring this man's *blood* upon us

6) Acts 13:44
   Almost the *whole city* gathered together.

7) Acts 15:21
   Moses has had in every city those who preach him.

8) Acts 22:3
   at the feet of Gamaliel

B. *Synecdoche* is the figure of speech by which the whole of a thing is put for the part, or a part for the whole, an individual for a class or a class for an individual, or an attribute for the whole. In the following tell what the relationship is and give the meaning of the passage.

Example: Luke 1:46
  My soul magnifies the Lord
    Soul is substituted for the person of which it is a part.
    Meaning — I magnify the Lord.

1) Luke 1:27
   Joseph, of the *house* of David

2) Luke 2:38
   to all who were looking for the redemption of *Jerusalem.*

3) Luke 3:6
   And all *flesh* shall see the salvation of God.

4) Luke 12:19
   and I will say to my *soul*

5) Acts 2:26
   My *tongue* rejoiced.

6) Acts 5:9
   Hark, the *feet* of those who have buried your husband are at the door.

7) Rom. 16:4
   who risked their *necks* for my life

C. "A *hyperbole* is an exaggeration for effect, not meant to be taken literally" (Webster). Since, in many cases, hyperboles cannot be translated literally into another language without giving a wrong idea, one must determine the actual nonfigurative meaning.

   Example: Matt. 11:18
      For John came neither eating nor drinking . . . .
         If translated literally this would not be true. Rather, the idea to be conveyed is that "John didn't eat at banquets or drink strong drink."

What meaning is being conveyed by the following hyperbolic phrases?

1) Mark 6:5
   And he could do *no mighty works* there.

2) John 3:32
   yet *no one* receives his testimony

3) John 12:19
   The world has gone after him.

4) John 21:25
   The world itself could not contain the books . . . .

5) Acts 17:6
   These men who have *turned the world upside down.*

6) Rom. 7:9
   Sin revived and I *died.*

7) 1 John 3:15
   Any one who hates his brother is *a murderer.*

D. "A *euphemism* is the use of a less direct word or phrase for one considered offensive" (Webster). Euphemisms vary from language to language. No attempt should be made to translate these literally, although some may be translated by corresponding euphemisms in the receptor language. What is the meaning of the euphemistic phrase in the following?

Example: Acts 13:36
   David . . . fell asleep, and was laid with his fathers.
   The natural meaning is "David died and was buried with his ancestors."

1) Mark 9:7
   A *voice* came out of the cloud.

2) Acts 1:25
   Judas turned aside, to *go to his own place.*

3) Acts 7:60
   And when he had said this, he *fell asleep.*
   (check context)

4) Acts 22:22
   Away with such a fellow *from the earth!*

5) Luke 2:5
   Mary was *with child.*

E. *Source-language idioms.* What are the meanings of the following source-language idioms? Study the context if necessary.

Example: Acts 18:6
   Your blood be upon your heads!
   You yourselves must take the blame for it! (TEV)

1) Matt. 5:2
He opened his mouth and taught them.

2) Mark 10:5
for your hardness of heart

3) Acts 11:22
News of this came to the ears of the church.

4) Acts 17:5
They set the city in an uproar.

5) Mark 10:22
his countenance fell

6) Luke 17:13
(They) lifted up their voices.

7) Mark 9:1
Some will not taste death.

8) 1 Pet. 1:13
Gird up your minds!

F. *Symbolic actions.* Study each of the following and give a suggested translation with reasons supporting your rendition.

Example: Matt. 27:39
Those who passed by derided him, wagging their heads and saying . . . .
In Chol (Mexico) wagging your head from side to side indicates an emphatic "No!" and wagging it up and down signifies joy. Since "wagging their heads" would give a wrong meaning, the following substitution was made: They reviled him, and showing disgust, they said . . . .

1) Luke 10:13
If the mighty works done in you had been done in Tyre and Sidon, they would have repented long ago, sitting in sackcloth and ashes.
Aguaruna: The action of sitting in sackcloth and ashes is unknown.

2) Acts 22:23

And as they cried out and waved their garments and threw dust into the air

Chol: Both actions are without significance unless explained.

3) Mark 7:3

The Jews do not eat unless they wash their hands, observing the tradition of the elders.

The language helper indicated that he thought the reason they washed their hands was so they would not get sick.

4) Matt. 3:11

He who is coming after me is mightier than I, whose sandals I am not worthy to carry.

Palantla Chinantec: The language helper interpreted this action as some kind of a trick, or a way to bother someone.

5) Acts 13:16

Paul stood up, and motioning with his hand . . .

Papago: Orators gain attention with the opening words of their address, not by motions and so the language helper wondered why Paul was motioning with his hand.

6) Mark 14:63

The high priest tore his mantle, and said, . . .

Tewa: the language helper could see no reason why the high priest would do this.

7) Acts 9:37

And when they had washed her, they laid her in an upper room.

Machigenga: The dead body is touched as little as possible, often being thrown into a river for disposal. It would hardly seem possible that they would wash her if she were really dead.

8) Mark 6:11

When you leave, shake off the dust that is on your feet for a testimony against them.

Aguaruna: The action seems strange because they live in the rain forest where desert dust is unknown. The symbolic significance would be carried out through loud conversation not by an act of shaking off of dust.

9) Luke 18:13

But the tax collector would not even lift up his eyes to heaven, but beat his breast, saying, . . .

Mesquital Otomi: This action could only mean that he was angry.

CHAPTER 8

The Nature of Metaphor and Simile

TEXT: Beekman-Callow, 1974, chapter 8

ADDITIONAL READING:

Aulie, Wilbur, 1957, "Figures of Speech in the Chol New Testament," *TBT* 8/3, 109-13

Beekman, John, 1969, "Metaphor and Simile," *NOT* 31:1-22

Morgan, G. Campbell, 1943, *The Parables and Metaphors of our Lord*, London: Marshall, Morgan & Scott Ltd.

Nida, Eugene A., 1950, "Translation or Paraphrase," *TBT* 1/3, 97-106

Nida, 1964, 219-21

A. "A *simile* is an explicit comparison in which one item of the comparison (the 'image') carries a number of components of meaning of which usually only one is contextually relevant to and shared by the second item (the 'topic')" (Beekman-Callow, 1974, 127).

Identify the shared component that is in focus as the basis of the simile in the following:

Example: Mark 4:31

It (the kingdom of God) is like a grain of mustard seed.

Shared component in focus: The smallness of the seed, which grows into a large bush, and the smallness of the beginning of the kingdom of God, which becomes large.

1) Rev. 3:3

I will come like a thief.

2) Matt. 3:16

He saw the Spirit of God descending like a dove, and alighting on him.

3) Matt. 17:20

If you have faith as a grain of mustard seed

4) Matt. 28:3

His appearance was like lightning.

5) Luke 13:21

It is like leaven which a woman took and hid in three measures of meal.

6) Luke 7:32

They are like children sitting in the market place and calling to one another.

7) 1 Pet. 1:19

(You were ransomed) with the precious blood of Christ, like that of a lamb without blemish or spot.

B. "A *metaphor* is an implicit comparison in which one item of the comparison (the 'image') carries a number of components of meaning of which usually only one is contextually relevant to and shared by the second item (the 'topic')" (Beekman-Callow, 1974, 127).

One cannot adequately translate some metaphors until he has determined the component of meaning that is in focus in the metaphor. Identify and explain the shared component that is the basis of the metaphor in the following:

Example: James 3:6

The tongue is a *fire.*

Component of destruction — fire ruins things, what we say ruins people.

1) Matt. 4:19

I will make you *fishers* of men.

2) Rom. 6:2

How can we who *died* to sin still live in it?

3) John 1:29

Behold, the *Lamb* of God, who takes away the sin of the world!

4) Acts 15:10

Now therefore why do you make trial of God by putting a *yoke upon the neck* of the disciples?

C. *Identifying topic, image, and point of similarity.* Every simile and metaphor consists of three parts: the topic, the image, and the point of similarity (the shared component of meaning). Identify these three parts in each of the following:

Example: Isaiah 53:6

All we like sheep have gone astray.

topic — we
image — sheep
point of similarity — gone astray

1) Heb. 11:12

From one man were born descendants as many as the stars of heaven.

2) Heb. 4:12

The word of God is sharper than any two-edged sword.

3) John 6:35

I am the bread of life.

4) John 10:9

I am the door.

5) Mark 1:17

I will make you become fishers of men.

6) John 5:35

(John) was a burning and shining lamp.

7) Heb. 6:19

We have this as a sure and steadfast anchor of the soul.

8) James 4:14

You are a mist that appears for a little time and then vanishes.

D. *Dead versus live metaphors.* A difference must be made between *dead metaphors,* those which are just a part of the idiomatic constructions of the lexicon of the language, and the *live metaphors,* those which are constructed on the spot to teach or illustrate. Study the following and decide whether you think the metaphor being used is a live metaphor or a dead one.

    Examples: Luke 1:42
        . . . and blessed is the fruit of your womb.
        an idiom (dead metaphor) which means "blessed is your child" and the metaphorical construction does not need to be kept.

John 10:7
    I am the door . . .
    a live metaphor which Jesus was using to teach. The image should be kept, making whatever adjustment is needed to carry the right meaning.

1) Acts 4:8
    Peter, *filled* with the Holy Spirit, said . . . .

2) Matt. 3:8
    Bear fruit that befits repentance.

3) Acts 17:6
    These men who have *turned the world upside down.*

4) Mark 14:27
    Jesus said to them, "You will all *fall away.*"

5) Matt. 4:19
    I will make you *fishers of men.*

6) Col. 1:10
    bearing fruit in every good work

7) John 8:44
    and the *father* of lies

8) Matt. 7:6
    "Do not give *dogs* what is holy; and do not throw your *pearls* before *swine.*"

E. *Meanings of dead metaphors (idioms).* The following are *dead metaphors*, idioms of the source language. What is the actual meaning of these idioms?

Example: Mark 5:22
> Jairus seeing him, he *fell at his feet.*
>> Aguaruna: Seeing him, he kneeled before him.

1) Luke 1:17
to *turn the hearts* of the fathers to the children

2) Acts 4:32
Those who believed *were of one heart and soul.*

3) Acts 2:35
till I *make* thy enemies *a stool for thy feet*

4) Luke 1:66
and all who heard them *laid them up in their hearts*

5) Acts 6:7
And the word of God *increased.*

6) Rom. 15:12
root of Jesse

7) John 13:18
has *lifted his heel* against me

8) Acts 9:1
Saul, still *breathing threats and murder* against the disciples

9) 1 Cor. 3:1
address you as *men of the flesh*

10) 1 Cor. 14:9
For you will be *speaking into the air.*

CHAPTER 9

Translating Metaphors and Similes

TEXT: Beekman-Callow, 1974, chapter 9

ADDITIONAL READING: (See additional reading for chapter 8 of this manual.)

Metaphors may be translated by a) the metaphorical form being retained in the RL; b) shifting to a simile; c) using non-figurative expressions; or d) a combination of these above three possibilities (Beekman-Callow, 1974, 145).

A. *Making explicit the three parts of a metaphor.* Assume that in translating Ephesians 6:10-17 you will need to make explicit the implied information of all live metaphors. First identify the three parts of the metaphor. Then rewrite the passage suggesting how you might make the implied information explicit.

Example: Matt. 23:24
You blind guides
topic — you
image — blind guides
similarity — cause others to error
You are like blind guides because you are in error and you lead people into error.

B. *Changing metaphors to similes.* "In Navajo one cannot speak of people 'being hungry and thirsty for righteousness' (Matthew 5:6). On the other hand, one can say 'like hungering and thirsting, they desire righteousness,' in which case a simile proves to be the real equivalent of the metaphor" (Nida, 1964, 220). The following are *live metaphors*, the form of which preferably should be retained in the translation. Change each of them to a simile without adding the grounds of the comparison.

Example: Acts 2:20
   The moon shall be turned to blood.
      The moon shall become like blood.

1) John 6:35
   Jesus said to them, "I am the *bread of life*."

2) John 14:6
   Jesus said to him, "I am the *way*."

3) John 10:11
   I am the *good shepherd*.

4) John 15:1
   I am the *true vine,* and my Father is the *vinedresser*.

5) John 1:29
   "Behold, the *Lamb of God,* who takes away the sin of the world!"

6) Matt. 5:13
   You are the *salt of the earth*.

7) Matt. 5:14
   You are the *light of the world*.

8) John 5:35
   He was a *burning and shining lamp*.

C. *Changing to a nonfigurative form.* Sometimes it may be necessary, or preferable, to use a nonfigurative form to translate a metaphor or simile. Dead metaphors should always be rendered nonfiguratively. Rewrite each of the following in a nonfigurative manner.

Example: Mark 1:17
   I will make you become fishers of men.
      You have been working catching fish, now I will give you a new work making disciples for me.

1) Matt. 17:20
   If you have faith as a grain of mustard

2) Luke 2:35
   A sword will pierce through your own soul also.

3) Philemon 2
   Archippus, our fellow soldier

4) Heb. 6:19
We have this as a sure and steadfast anchor of the soul.

5) Heb. 2:7
Thou hast crowned him with glory and honor.

D. *Review.* Identify the figure of speech that occurs in each of the following and tell what kind it is.

Example: 1 Cor. 3:9
For we are fellow workmen for God; you are God's building.
Building is a metaphor.

1) Matt. 2:6
And you, O Bethlehem, in the land of Judah, are by no means least among the rulers of Judah.

2) Mark 6:11
if any place will not receive you and they refuse to hear you

3) Mark 12:43
This poor widow has put in more than all those who are contributing to the treasury.

4) John 6:33
For the bread of God is that which comes down from heaven and gives life to the world.

5) Acts 6:15
And gazing at him all who sat in the council saw that his face was like the face of an angel.

6) 1 Cor. 4:8
Already you are filled! Already you have become rich! Without us you would have become kings!

7) Eph. 6:17
And take the helmet of salvation, and the sword of the Spirit, which is the word of God.

8) Col. 1:20
through him to reconcile to himself all things, whether on earth or in heaven, making peace by the blood of his cross

9) James 5:12
Do not swear, either by heaven or by earth or with any other oath.

CHAPTER 10

Concordance and Meanings in Context

TEXT: Beekman-Callow, 1974, chapter 10

ADDITIONAL READING:

Bratcher, Robert G., 1961, *Old Testament Quotations in the New Testament*, United Bible Societies, London

Hess, Harwood, "A Study of glōssa in the New Testament," 1964, *TBT* 15/2, 93-96

Nida and Taber, 1969, 15-22

Richert, Ernest, 1965, "Multiple Meanings and Concordance," *NOT* 16:3

"Concordance within a document occurs when the same word or expression is used repeatedly to refer to the same specific concept . . . . Concordance between an original document and its translation occurs when a word or expression in the source document is translated in each of its occurrences with the same word or expression wherever contextual usage warrants" (Beekman-Callow, 1974, 152).

A. *Spirit.* In the following passages the word "spirit" occurs in each verse. However, since each occurrence represents a different sense of the word "spirit," this is *pseudo* concordance and not *real* concordance. Match the five senses of the word "spirit" listed below with the verses in which the sense is used. In some languages each sense will be translated by a different word or phrase.

Example: Mark 5:13
The unclean *spirits* came out and entered the swine.
The sense is a demon, evil spirit.

a) demon, evil spirit
b) angel, good spirit
c) Spirit of God, Holy Spirit

d) part of the human personality
e) ghost, spirit of a dead person

1) Heb. 1:14
Are they not all ministering spirits sent forth to serve?

2) Acts 2:4
They began to speak in other tongues, as the Spirit gave them utterance.

3) Matt. 26:41
The spirit indeed is willing, but the flesh is weak.

4) Acts 16:16
We were met by a slave girl who had a spirit of divination and brought her owners much gain by soothsaying.

5) Luke 24:37
But they were startled and frightened, and supposed that they saw a spirit.

6) Gal. 3:2
Did you receive the Spirit by the works of the law, or by hearing with faith?

7) Luke 1:80
And the child grew and became strong in spirit.

B. *Tongue.* The word "tongue" has many senses in Greek. It is not likely that it will have all of these same senses in another language. Study each of the following to decide what the meaning of "tongue" is in the passage. After you have done this, look up the same passage in TEV and see how "tongue" has been translated there. The TEV has not kept the pseudo concordance of the Greek.

Example: 1 Pet. 3:10
Let him refrain his *tongue* from evil.
Tongue means to speak.
TEV uses *speak*.

1) Luke 1:64
And immediately his mouth was opened and his tongue loosed.

2) Luke 16:24
Send Lazarus to dip the end of his finger in water and cool my tongue.

3) 1 John 3:18
   Little children, let us not love in word, neither in tongue;
   but in deed and truth. (KJV)

4) 1 Cor. 12:10
   to another the ability to distinguish between spirits, to
   another various kinds of tongues, to another the interpreta-
   tion of tongues.

5) Rom. 14:11
   Every knee shall bow to me, and every tongue shall give
   praise to God.

6) Rev. 16:10
   Its kingdom was in darkness; men gnawed their tongues in
   anguish.

7) Acts 2:26
   Therefore my heart was glad, and my tongue rejoiced.

8) Rev. 5:9
   Thou wast slain and by thy blood didst ransom men for God
   from every tribe and tongue and people and nation.

9) Acts 2:3
   And there appeared to them tongues as of fire.

10) James 3:6
    And the tongue is a fire. The tongue is an unrighteous
    world among our members.

C. *House.* In each of the following verses the word "house"
occurs. The Greek word "house" is used in many senses. What
is the sense in each of the following occurrences? After you have
decided what sense is used, look the verse up in the *Living Bible*
and TEV and compare the translation of "house" with that given
in the KJV below.

Example: Matt. 10:6
   But go rather to the lost sheep of the house of Israel.
   House means *people.*
   TEV people, LB people

1) Matt. 9:6
   Arise, take up thy bed, and go unto thine house.

2) Luke 1:27

Gabriel was sent to a virgin espoused to a man whose name was Joseph, of the house of David; and the virgin's name was Mary.

3) Acts 16:31

And they said, Believe on the Lord Jesus Christ, and thou shalt be saved, and thy house.

4) Acts 7:20

In which time Moses was born and nourished up in his father's house three months

5) Matt. 12:4

how he entered into the house of God, and did eat the shewbread

D. *Comparing versions.* Using rsv, tev, and neb, study each of the following groups of passages to see how the Greek word has been translated.

1) List the different ways that *katargeō* ("to render useless") is rendered:

Luke 13:7	Rom. 3:3	Rom. 6:6
Rom. 7:2	1 Cor. 2:6	1 Cor. 13:8
1 Cor. 15:24	2 Cor. 3:7	2 Cor. 3:14
Gal. 5:4	2 Thess. 2:8	Heb. 2:14

2) List the different ways *katartizō* ("to restore") is rendered:

Matt. 4:21	Heb. 10:5	1 Peter 5:10
Luke 6:40	1 Cor. 1:10	Heb. 13:21
Gal. 6:1	1 Thess. 3:10	

3) List the different ways *parakaleō* ("beseech") is rendered:

Matt. 2:18	Matt. 8:31	Acts 2:40
Matt. 26:53	2 Cor. 6:1	Acts 24:4

4) List the different ways *agōn* ("contest") is rendered:

Phil. 1:30	Col. 2:1	Heb. 12:1
1 Thess. 2:2	1 Tim. 6:12	

5) List the different ways *akoē* ("hearing") is rendered:

Matt. 4:24	Matt. 13:14	Matt. 24:6
Mark 7:35	John 12:38	1 Thess. 2:13

6) List the different ways *achri* ("up to a point") is rendered:

Acts 28:15	Acts 11:5	1 Cor. 4:11
Luke 4:13	Acts 13:11	Acts 20:6

7) List the different ways *astheneia* ("weakness") is rendered:

Matt. 8:17	Luke 5:15	1 Tim. 5:23
Acts 28:9	Rom. 6:19	Gal. 4:13

E. *Old and New Testament Concordance.* "In translating the New Testament, including the quotations contained therein, one must strive for an accurate representation of what the New Testament writings meant to their readers. It is not the business of the translator to 'correct' the New Testament by introducing, for example, a translation from the Hebrew Masoretic text if the New Testament writer followed the Septuagint or some other rendering" (Bratcher, 1961, vii). New Testament writers did not adhere to strict concordant usage of Old Testament passages.

Study the following and identitfy the changes that were made in each passage.

Example: Isa. 7:14
Behold, a virgin shall conceive, and bear a son, and shall call his name Immanuel. (KJV)

Matt. 1:23
Behold, a virgin shall conceive and bear a son, and his name shall be called Immanuel.
Active *shall call* was changed to passive *shall be called.*

1) Joel 2:28
And it shall come to pass afterward, that I will pour out my spirit on all flesh; your sons and your daughters shall prophesy, your old men shall dream dreams, and your young men shall see visions.

Acts 2:17
And in the last days it shall be, God declares, that I will pour out my Spirit upon all flesh, and your sons and your daughters shall prophesy, and your young men shall see visions, and your old men shall dream dreams.

2) Joel 2:29
Even upon the menservants and maidservants in those days, I will pour out my Spirit.

Acts 2:18
Yea, and on my menservants and my maidservants in those days, I will pour out my Spirit and they shall prophesy.

3) Isa. 6:9
Go, and say to this people

Acts 28:26
Go to this people and say

4) Isa. 6:9
Hear and hear, but do not understand, see and see, but do not perceive

Mark 4:12
so that they may indeed see but not perceive, and may indeed hear but not understand

5) Isa. 6:10
and turn and be healed

Mark 4:12
turn again and be forgiven

6) Ps. 78:2
I will utter dark sayings from of old.

Matt. 13:35
I will utter what has been hidden since the foundation of the world.

7) Deut. 24:1
He writes her a bill of divorce and puts it in her hand and sends her out of his house, and she departs out of his house.

Matt. 19:7
to give a certificate of divorce and put her away

8) Ps. 118:22
The stone which the builders rejected has become the chief cornerstone.

Acts 4:11
This is the stone which was rejected by the builders but which has become the head of the corner.

9) Exod. 3:10a
Come, I will send you to Pharaoh.

Acts 7:34b
And now come, I will send you to Egypt.

CHAPTER 11

Collocational Clash

TEXT: Beekman-Callow, 1974, chapter 11

ADDITIONAL READING:

Ballard, D. Lee, Jr., 1968, "Studying the Receptor Language Lexicon," *NOT* 29, 11-15

Beekman, John, 1968, "Eliciting Vocabulary, Meaning, and Collocations," *NOT* 29:1-11

Evans, Helen M., 1954, "Experiences in Translating the New Testament in Kui," *TBT* 5/1, 44

Headland, Thomas N., 1973, "A Method for Recording Formal Elicitation," *NOT* 50:22-27

Hollenbach, Barbara E., 1970, "Some Limitations of the Question Technique," *NOT* 36:26-28

Hudspith, Mrs. T. E., 1952, "Notes on the Translation of the New Testament in Bolivian Quechua," *TBT* 3/2, 66-68

McIntosh, Angus, 1961, "Patterns and Ranges," *Language* 37/3, 325-27

Nida, 1947, 276-79

Nida, 1964, 70-119

Pallesen, Kemp, 1970, "More on Elicitation," *NOT* 36:20-26

Richert, Ernest L., 1965, "Native Reaction as a Guide to Meaningful Translation," *NOT with Drills*, 44-47

Williams, Kenneth L., 1965, "Checking Translations for Wrong Meaning," *NOT with Drills*, 38-44

"In a collocational clash there is a conflict of meaning components within the text carried not by the grammar but by the lexical choices made" (Beekman-Callow, 1974, 162).

95

"Each word and idiom in a language is selective with respect to the company it keeps, and the list of permissible company defines its *collocational range*" (Ibid., 162-63).

A. *Identifying potential collocational clashes.* "In Acts 3:7 we first translated 'ankle bones received strength' by the Quechua phrase 'his ankle bones took hold on strength.' The verb 'to take hold of' is the Quechua equivalent of 'to receive,' but the phrase 'to take hold of strength' is not satisfactory Quechua. The natural and normal way of expressing this idea is 'the ankle bones were strengthened.' Accordingly, we changed our earlier rendering in order to express the idea in the proper Quechua manner.

"A similar problem occurred in Acts 28:3 in the phrase 'laid them on the fire , . . .' At first we translated more or less automatically 'put them on the fire.' But then we realized that no Quechua would speak that way. He would say *enkhashajtin* meaning 'to feed the fire'" (Hudspith, 66).

Which combinations of words in the following passages are not used in their primary meaning and therefore may set up a collocational clash if translated literally into another language?

Example: John 11:32
Mary, when she came where Jesus was and saw him, fell at his feet, saying , . . .
The words 'fell at his feet' if taken in their primary meaning might mean she tripped over his feet and fell.
(Campa, of Peru, says, 'She kneeled to him.')

1) John 4:1
Now when the Lord knew that the Pharisees had heard that Jesus was making and baptizing more disciples than John . . . .

2) John 12:30
Jesus answered, "This voice has come for your sake, not for mine."

3) Acts 6:7
And the word of God increased; and the number of the disciples multiplied greatly in Jerusalem, and a great many of the priests were obedient to the faith.

4) 1 Tim. 2:8
I desire then that in every place the men should pray lifting holy hands without anger or quarreling.

B. *Basis for collocational clashes.* The italicized words in the following are not being used in their primary meaning but in an extended usage. What is probably the primary meaning of the italicized word or phrase? Explain the basis of the extension of meaning as used in English, which, however, is not allowed in the language cited.

Example: John 16:6
Sorrow has filled your hearts.
Shipibo (of Peru) says, "In your hearts you are very sad." The primary meaning of *fill* is to put liquid, or other non-solid substances into a container. This has been extended to include abstracts such as *sorrow*.

1) Matt. 8:34
All the *city* came out to *meet* Jesus.
Kui, India: everyone went out to see him.

2) John 3:33
set his *seal* to this, that God is true
Campa, Peru: They really say about God, 'He is true.'

3) John 3:35
has *given* all things *into his hand*.
Campa, Peru: has allowed him to rule over all.

4) John 8:51
He will never *see* death.
Aguaruna, Peru: He will not die.

5) John 9:16
There was a *division* among them.
Aguaruna, Peru: Arguingly they talked.

C. *Basis for collocational clashes, continued.* What restriction is probably the basis for changing the italicized words in the following passages?

Example: John 16:22
No one will *take* your joy *from* you.
Hopi: No one will *make* your joy *end*.
Take occurs with concrete nouns, not abstract nouns such as joy.

1) Matt. 9:2
When Jesus *saw* their faith he said . . .
Sierra Zapotec: Jesus *understood* that they had faith.

2) Acts 2:41
So those who *received* his word were baptized.
Isthmus Mixe: So those who *believed* Peter's words . . . .

3) Acts 7:18
till there *arose* over Egypt another King
Aguaruna: another King *replaced* (the other one) in Egypt.

4) Acts 7:16
and *laid* in the tomb that Abraham had bought
Morelos Aztec: *buried* their bodies in Abraham's grave

5) Acts 9:31
The church throughout all Judea was *built up*
Pame: *became strong* as they believed

6) Acts 13:22
He *raised* up David to be their king.
Aguaruna: 'That he be chief' saying, he *named* David.

7) Acts 15:5
and to charge them to *keep* the law of Moses
Huave: to be told that they are *to do* even *as stated* in the law of Moses

8) Acts 22:3
but *brought up* at the feet of Gamaliel
Morelos Aztec: *studied* with Professor Gamaliel

D. *Elicitation.* If possible, the student should find some non-English speaker and practice the elicitation procedure suggested in the last half of chapter 17 of Beekman-Callow, 1974.

CHAPTER 12

Lexical Equivalence Across Languages — When Concepts Are Shared

Text: Beekman-Callow, 1974, chapter 12

Additional Reading:

Grimes, Joseph E., 1966, "Sin," *NOT* 22:11-16

Mansen, Richard, 1971, "Understanding the World of the Supernatural," *NOT* 39:3-12

Moore, Bruce, 1972, "Doublets," *NOT* 43

Nida, 1947, 130-240

Nida, 1964, 171-77, 213-23, 230-31

A. *Semantically complex words.* "A word can symbolize a large or a small area of experience. Since words are semantically complex, it is often necessary to 'unpack' the bundle of components when translating into another language and to use a phrase or clause as an equivalent" (Beekman-Callow, 1974, 179). In the passages that follow, some of the semantically complex words have been italicized. Rewrite the passage, using a phrase or clause to replace the italicized word, thus "unpacking" the meaning components.

Example: Mark 14:70
But again he denied it.
Aguaruna: Again he said, "I don't know him."

1) Acts 27:16
And running under the *lee* of a small *island* called Cauda, we managed with difficulty to secure the boat.

2) Rom. 8:26
The Spirit himself *intercedes* for us.

3) John 10:2
   He who enters by the door is the *shepherd* of the sheep.

4) Luke 7:34
   Behold a *glutton* and a *drunkard*.

5) Luke 8:1
   Soon afterward he went on through *cities* and *villages*.

6) Acts 16:25
   Paul and Silas were *praying* and singing hymns to God.

7) Acts 16:39
   So they came and *apologized* to them.

8) Acts 2:45
   They sold their *possessions* and distributed them to all.

9) John 15:1
   My Father is the *vinedresser*.

10) John 12:43
    They loved the *praise* of men more than the *praise* of God.

B. *Semantic doublets.* "The use of synonyms may be of special difficulty to the translator. This is the use of two (or more) synonymous words or expressions together in what may be termed a 'doublet,' or a 'rhetorical parallelism.' In the particular context, there is no focal difference in meaning between the terms used; rather, they represent a single concept. However, the doublet form may be used to emphasize the idea, or to modify the area of meaning slightly, or it may be a type of stylistic redundancy" (Beekman-Callow, 1974, 181).

Identify the doublet in each of the following passages.

Example: 1 John 3:18
   Little children, let us not love in word or speech but in deed and in truth.

   Word or speech; and *in deed and in truth* are both doublets.

1) Matt. 5:12
   Rejoice and be glad, for your reward is great in heaven, for so men persecuted the prophets who were before you.

2) Matt. 12:19

He will not wrangle or cry aloud, nor will any one hear his voice in the streets.

3) Matt. 23:37

O Jerusalem, Jerusalem, killing the prophets and stoning those who are sent to you! How often would I have gathered your children together as a hen gathers her brood under her wings, and you would not!

4) Mark 14:33

And he took with him Peter and James and John, and began to be greatly distressed and troubled.

5) Mark 15:34

And at the ninth hour Jesus cried with a loud voice, "My God, my God, why hast thou forsaken me?"

6) Luke 1:6

And they were both righteous before God, walking in all the commandments and ordinances of the Lord blameless.

7) 2 Thess. 3:2

and that we may be delivered from wicked and evil men

8) James 1:17

Every good endowment and every perfect gift is from above, coming down from the Father of lights with whom there is no variation or shadow due to change.

9) James 5:11

Behold, we call those happy who were steadfast. You have heard of the steadfastness of Job, and you have seen the purpose of the Lord, how the Lord is compassionate and merciful.

C. *Negating an Antonym* is one way of handling a positive term for which there is no literal counterpart. Rewrite the following using a negated antonym for the italicized word.

Example: Acts 9:16

I will show him *how much he must* suffer.

Bila'an (Philippines): I will show him it is not possible that he will not suffer much.

1) Matt. 13:48
   (They) sorted the food into vessels but threw away the *bad*.

2) Acts 19:22
   He himself *stayed* in Asia for a while.

3) Mark 3:25
   And if a house is *divided against itself*, that house will not be able to stand.

4) 2 Cor. 7:12
   It was not on account of the one who did the *wrong*.

5) Mark 14:70
   But again he *denied* it.

6) 2 Cor. 6:17
   I will *welcome* you.

7) Luke 16:9
   They may receive you into the *eternal* habitations.

8) Luke 11:21
   When a *strong* man, fully armed, guards his own palace.

9) Mark 14:4
   Why was the ointment thus *wasted*?

10) Matt. 10:22
    He who *endures* to the end will be saved.

D. *Litotes* is affirmation made by the negation or belittlement or understatement of an opposite idea. Usually it is used for emphasis. What is the natural meaning of the following?

   Example: Acts 1:5
   before many days (RSV) really means "in a few days" (TEV)

1) Mark 9:41
   (He) shall by no means lose his reward.

2) Mark 12:34
   You are not far from the kingdom of God.

3) Luke 1:37
   For with God nothing will be impossible.

4) John 20:17
Jesus said to her, "Do not hold me."

5) Acts 20:12
not a little comforted

6) Acts 21:39
a citizen of no mean city

7) Acts 26:19
not disobedient

8) Rom. 4:19
He did not weaken in faith.

9) 2 Cor. 1:8
We do not want you to be ignorant.

10) 2 Cor. 11:5
I am not in the least inferior to these superlative apostles.

11) Gal. 4:12
You did me no wrong.

12) Eph. 1:16
I do not cease to give thanks for you.

E. *Reciprocal equivalent.* In the reciprocal equivalent, the noun that has been the subject assumes a different role in the sentence, and another noun becomes the subject. The verb, however, is different, in that it is the reciprocal but still represents the same event. Rewrite the following, using a reciprocal equivalent.

Example: 1 Cor. 11:23
For I have *received* from the Lord that which I also delivered to you.
What the Lord gave to me is what I also gave to you.

1) Acts 24:26
He hoped that money would be *given* him by Paul.

2) Matt. 28:18
All authority has been *given* unto me . . . .

3) Matt. 4:12
Now when he *heard* that John had been arrested, he withdrew.

4) Luke 1:45
Blessed is she who believed what was *spoken* to her from the Lord.

5) Mark 13:5
Take heed that no one *leads* you *astray.*

F. *Generic-specific.* Review chapter 4, section D of this manual.

G. *Changing to nonfigurative usage.* In each of the following the figurative expression is italicized. Rewrite the passage using a nonfigurative expression.

Example: Matt. 10:34
I have not come to bring peace, but *a sword.*
Mazahua: There will be dissension among the people.

1) John 4:35
Lift up your eyes, and see how the fields are already white for harvest.

2) John 4:47
He was *at the point of death.*

3) John 6:46
If you had believed *Moses,* you would believe me.

4) John 6:63
It is the spirit that *gives life,* the *flesh* is of no avail.

5) John 7:30
So they sought to arrest him; but no one *laid hands on him.*

6) John 8:37
You seek to kill me, because my word *finds no place in you.*

CHAPTER 13

Lexical Equivalence Across Languages — When Things or Events Are Unknown

TEXT: Beekman-Callow, 1974, chapter 13

ADDITIONAL READING:

Beekman, John, 1965, "Lexical Equivalence Involving Consideration of Form and Function," *NOT with Drills*, 83-123

Dodd, C. H., 1962, "Some Problems of New Testament Translation," *TBT* 13/3 145-57

Edgerton, Faye, 1962, "Some Translation Problems in Navajo," *TBT* 13/1, 25-33

Kelley, L. G., 1970, "Cultural Consistency in Translation," *TBT* 21/4, 170-75

Nida, Eugene A., 1955, "Problems in Translating the Scriptures into Shilluk, Anuak and Nuer," *TBT* 6/2, 55-63

Nida, 1947, 241-79

Nida, 1964, 165-77

Olson, Ronald, 1972, "Those Pesky Loan Words," *NOT* 46:28-31

Reyburn, William D., 1969, "Cultural Equivalence and Non-equivalences in Translation #I," *TBT* 20/4, 158-67

Reyburn, William D., 1970, "Cultural Equivalence and Non-equivalences in Translation #II," *TBT* 21/1, 26-35

Wheatley, James, 1973, "Political Structure and Translation," *NOT* 48:27-32

A. *Form versus function.* In each of the following, a word in the passage is italicized. In the comment about a word or phrase in another language that word or phrase is also italicized. Decide which type of correspondence there is between the two words as to form and function: either (1) same form and same function,

(2) same form but different function, (3) different form but same function, or (4) no correspondence of either form or function. Determining such correspondence will help decide if the word can be used in a given textual situation.

Example: Acts 8:28
(He) was returning; seated in his *chariot*.
Zapoteco: travel in *ox carts*
Form is different, function is the same.

1) Matt. 21:33
There was a householder who planted a vineyard and built a *tower*.

Aguarunas build *towers* if they have enemies who are expected to attack. They then run from their house to the tower when the enemy approaches the house and thus have the advantage over the enemy.

2) Mark 12:10
The very *stone* which the builders rejected has become the head of the corner.

In the tropical forest of Peru, houses are not made of stone but of poles with palm thatch roofs. There is one *main pole* that is the center of the whole structure in some tribes.

3) Mark 15:17
Plaiting a *crown* of thorns they put it on him. (crown a symbol of royalty)

Many tribes wear crowns for ornamentation when they get dressed up to go visiting or to a fiesta.

4) John 6:35
Jesus said to them, "I am the *bread* of life."

Among the Chontal bread is made for special fiesta days only, but *tortillas* are the regular food used each day.

5) John 10:12
The *wolf* snatches them and scatters them (the sheep).

In the tropical forest there are no wolves, but there are *tigers* which steal domesticated animals.

6) John 11:17

Lazarus had already been in the *tomb* four days.

Aguarunas place the dead body on a *platform* in an abandoned house. This is called "the-place-where-one-is-left." The body is left there for months and food brought daily. A fire is kept burning at the foot. Eventually the bones are buried in a clay pot.

B. *Modified with a statement of function.* In the following, for the italicized word use a generic representation of form and make the function explicit.

Example: Matt. 12:9

synagogue

their meeting house (State of Mexico Otomi)

1) Mark 6:4

a *prophet* is not without honor

2) Luke 3:17

and to gather the wheat into his *granary*

3) John 10:1

he who does not enter the *sheepfold* by the door

4) John 10:2

He who enters by the door is the *shepherd* . . . .

5) John 15:1

My Father is the *vinedresser.*

6) Acts 5:18

They arrested the apostles and put them in the common *prison.*

7) Acts 5:20

Go and stand in the *temple* and speak.

8) Acts 5:21

Now the high priest came and called together the *council.*

9) Acts 21:34

He ordered him to be brought into the *barracks.*

10) Phil. 1:1

to all the saints and *deacons*

C. *Loan word modified with a classifier.* Assume that you will use a loan word for the word italicized in the following passages. What classifier would be needed to make the meaning clear?

Example: Luke 4:1
    And Jesus returned from the *Jordan*.
    And Jesus returned from the *Jordan River*.

1) John 1:51
You will see the *angels* of God ascending.

2) John 11:1
Now a certain man was ill, Lazarus of *Bethany*.

3) John 2:5
Six stone jars were standing there, for the *Jewish* rites of purification.

4) Luke 1:5
In the days of Herod, king of *Judea*.

5) Luke 6:17
A great multitude of people from all *Judea* and *Jerusalem* and the seacoast of *Tyre* and *Sidon* came to hear him.

D. *Loan word modified with a specification of form or function or both.* Assume that you are going to use a loan word for the word italicized in the following passages. What additional specification of form or function, or both form and function, might be needed?

Example: Mark 1:13
    He was tempted by Satan.
    Sambal (Philippines): He was tempted by *Satan, the ruler of the demons.*

1) John 1:41
We have found the *Messiah*.

2) Acts 23:6
One part were *Sadducees*.

3) John 3:1
Now there was a man of the *Pharisees*, named Nicodemus.

4) Acts 27:29
They let out four *anchors* from the stern.

5) James 3:3
We put *bits* into the mouths of horses that they may obey us.

E. *Cultural substitutes.* "In certain situations the translator may find that equivalence using a generic term or a loan word is impossible or impractical and may need to resort to the use of equivalence by cultural substitution. A cultural substitute is the use of a real-world referent from the receptor culture for an unknown referent of the original, both of the referents having the same *function*" (Beekman-Callow, 1974, 201).

Study the following passages to determine if the form of the italicized item is in focus and therefore must be retained or if the function is in focus and the form may be (1) dropped, (2) referred to generically, or (3) referred to with a cultural substitute.

Example: Matt. 28:3
His raiment was white as *snow.*
Form not in focus and may be dropped, only the intensity of the whiteness is in focus.

Mark 4:3 A sower went out to *sow.*
Form is in focus, that is, scattering of the seed.

1) Mark 4:29
He puts in the *sickle*, because the harvest has come.

2) Acts 4:27
Jesus, whom thou didst *anoint.*

3) Mark 14:3
A woman came with an alabaster *jar* of ointment of pure nard, and she broke the jar and poured it over his head.

4) Matt. 10:27
And what you hear whispered, proclaim upon the *housetops.*

5) Matt. 25:1
ten maidens who took their *lamps*

6) Matt. 25:3
They took no *oil* with them.

7) Matt. 23:37
I have gathered your children together as a *hen* gathers her brood under wings, and you would not!

8) Matt. 26:75
Before the *cock* crows, you will deny me three times.

9) Matt. 27:32
This man they compelled to carry his *cross.*

F. *Identifying lexical equivalence.* Study the translation made of each of the following passages. What adjustment was made as to form and function of the italicized word? Choose your answer from the following and write the letter on your answer sheet.

a) Same form, function made explicit
b) Form changed to more generic, function made explicit
c) Loan word plus classifier or descriptive phrase
d) Form omitted and function only retained
e) Another specific substituted

Example: Matt. 8:20
Foxes have holes, and birds of the air have nests.
Mazahua: coyotes
Answer: e, another specific was substituted

1) Acts 27:29
They let out four *anchors* from the stern
Northern Totonaco: weights, and thus they were able to make the boat stand . . .

2) Acts 27:29
They let out four *anchors* from the stern.
Chol: that which makes a boat stay

3) John 1:23
I am the voice of one crying in the *wilderness.*
Agta: where no people dwell

4) John 1:48
. . . under the *fig* tree I saw you.
Aguaruna: the tree called *ikuira* (Spanish: Higuera)

5) Acts 8:28
seated in his *chariot*
Sierra Otomi: cart pulled by horses

6) Acts 10:17
   made inquiry for *Simon's house*
   Palantla Chinanteco: where Simon lived

7) Acts 26:29
   except for these *chains*
   Northern Totonaco: not have their hands bound like me

REVIEW

A. *Identifying translation adjustments.* Identify as many translation adjustments that have been made in the following translation as you can. Compare with RSV or ASV.

John 6:1-14 (Chol)

[1]Afterwards Jesus crossed the Galilee Sea. Its name is also Tiberias. [2]Many went following Jesus because they saw the picture of his power which he showed on behalf of the sick ones. [3]Jesus went up into the mountains. There he sat with his learners. [4]It was near the day of the Pascua which the Jews celebrated. [5]Jesus looked, he saw men and women coming where he was. Jesus said to Philip, "How can we buy food for them to eat?" he said. [6]Jesus spoke these words because he wanted to see the heart of Philip how he would answer, because Jesus knew it himself (by himself) what he wanted to do. [7]Philip said, "It would not be enough, 200 denarii, in order that tortillas be purchased, in order that a little bit each eat," he said. [8]One of his learners whose name was Andrew, the younger brother of Simon Peter, said, [9]"Here is a boy. He has five units of food made of cebada (barley) and two fish. Is this enough for so many of us-inclusive?" he said. [10]Jesus said, "Tell the men and women to sit down. There is grass," he said. The men and women sat down. There were 5,000 men. [11]Jesus took the food. When he said thanks to God he tore it. He gave to his learners. The learners distributed it to the seated ones. Thus also the fish. They all ate however much they wanted. [12]When full, Jesus said to his learners, "Gather the pieces that are left so that not even a little bit will be lost." For this reason they gathered it. [13]They filled twelve baskets with the pieces of the five units of food which were left over after they had eaten. [14]Men saw the picture of his power that Jesus showed. They said, "It is true this is the prophet who was to come to earth," they said.

B. *Identifying translation adjustments.* Identify the adjustments that have been made in the following translations.

Example: John 2:1
there was a marriage

Shipibo: a certain man got married. For him to marry they made food.

Abstract noun to verb phrase and participants made more explicit.

1) John 2:3
They have no wine.
Aguaruna: There is no drink.

2) John 2:6
each holding twenty or thirty gallons
Chinanteco: each pot held about eight small waterpots

3) John 2:8
now draw some out
Chinanteco: dip up a little of that

4) John 2:8
the steward of the feast
Campa: the boss of the servants

5) John 2:12
went down to Capernaum
Tepehua: went to the town of Capernaum

6) John 2:13
The Passover of the Jews was at hand.
Chinanteco: Time was approaching for the Jews to make a feast, feast of the passing by of God's angel.

7) John 2:14
in the temple
Aguaruna: in the house for talking to God

8) John 2:19
destroy this temple
Isthmus Mixe: cause this temple to fall

9) John 3:3
he cannot see the kingdom of God
Chinanteco: God cannot rule over that one

10) John 3:4
Can he enter a second time into his mother's womb and be born?
Northern Totonac: He cannot enter into the womb of his mother to be born again.

C. *Identifying translation adjustments.* Identify the adjustment that has been made in each of the following translations.

Example: John 3:11
but you do not receive our testimony
Aguaruna: but you don't listen to what we tell
receive — collocational clash, words are *listened to*
our testimony — abstract noun changed to *what we tell*

1) John 3:14
Moses lifted up the serpent
Aguaruna: Moses put up high that made imitating a snake

2) John 3:15
have eternal life
Campa: he will keep on living

3) John 3:17
but that the world might be saved through him
Aguaruna: rather, 'that he save people' saying, he sent him.

4) John 3:19
and this is the judgment
Northern Totonac: for this reason they will be punished

5) John 3:23
at Aenon near Salim
Tepehua: in the town of Aenon near the town of Salim

6) John 3:26
They came to John.
Tepehua: John's disciples came to their teacher.

7) John 3:36
The Father loves the Son.
Aguaruna: God, our Father loves his son.

8) John 3:35
   but the wrath of God rests upon him
   Chinanteco: for God has already become angry with him

9) John 4:6
   Jacob's well was there.
   Aguaruna: There was a well which had been dug by Jacob.

CHAPTER 14

Multiple Functions of Grammatical Structures

TEXT: Beekman-Callow, 1974, chapter 14

ADDITIONAL READING:

Beekman, John, ed., 1965, *NOT with Drills*, 124-76

Beekman, John, 1965, "Extended Usage of Number and Person," *NOT* 19:1-10

Beekman, John, 1967, "Introduction to Skewing of the Lexical and Grammatical Hierarchies," *NOT* 23:1

Butler, Inez M., 1965, "Implicit Exclusiveness in Villa Alta Zapotec," *NOT* 16:4, 5

Butler, Inez M., 1967, "Use of Third Person for First Person in the Gospel of John," *NOT* 26:10-14

Davis, Marjorie, 1952, "Translating Nouns into the Cuicateco Language," *TBT* 3/1, 34-38

Greenlee, J. Harold, 1954, "New Testament Participles," *TBT* 5/3, 98-100

France, R. T., 1972, "The Exegesis of Greek Tenses in the New Testament," *NOT* 46:3-12

Law, Howard W., 1966, "Grammatical Equivalences in Bible Translating," *TBT* 17/3, 123-28

Lithgow, David, 1967, "Exclusiveness of Muyuw Pronouns," *NOT* 26:14

Lithgow, David, 1971, "Change of Subject in Muyuw," *NOT* 41:21-27

Lofthouse, W. F., 1955, " 'I' and 'We' in the Pauline Letters," *TBT* 6/2, 72-80 (Reprinted from *The Expository Times*, May 1953)

116 PROBLEM SOLVING IN BIBLE TRANSLATION

Lund, Nils Wilhelm, 1942, *Chiasmus in the New Testament*, Durham, N. C.: University of North Carolina Press

Nida, 1947, 241-76

Nida, Eugene A., 1955, "Problems in Translating the Scripture into Shilluk, Anuak and Nuer," *TBT* 6/2, 55-63

Nida, 1964, 57-69, 138-40

Pike, Eunice V., 1966, "Nonfocus of Person and Focus of Role," *NOT* 20:17, 18

Pike, Eunice V., 1967, "Skewing of the Lexical and Grammatical Hierarchy as it Affects Translation," *NOT* 23:1-3

Slocum, Marianna C., 1971, "A Positive Use for the Negative," *NOT* 42:17-19

Wonderly, William L., 1953, "Information-Correspondence and the Translation of Ephesians into Zoque," *TBT* 4/1, 14-21

SECTION 1. PASSIVE-ACTIVE

A. *Identifying passives and actives.* State whether the following verb phrases are passive or active.

Example: Mark 6:14
John the baptizer has been raised from the dead.
passive

1) John 1:45
Philip found Nathaniel, and said to him

2) 2 Cor. 1:6
If we are afflicted . . . if we are comforted

3) Acts 8:10
They all gave heed to him.

4) John 2:12
After this he went down to Capernaum.

5) John 1:6
There was a man sent from God.

6) Matt. 28:18
All authority has been given unto me.

7) John 1:29
The next day he saw Jesus coming toward him.

8) Acts 8:33
   For his life is taken up from the earth.

9) Mark 13:13
   You will be hated by all for my name's sake.

10) 1 John 4:9
    In this the love of God was made manifest among us.

B. *Changing passives to actives.* "Zoque has no regular equivalent of the passive voice. Certain active intransitive verbs are roughly equivalent to English passive verbs whose agent is unmarked. . . . But in most cases a transitive verb must be used, and a subject introduced even if no agent is present in the text" (Wonderly, 1953, 15).

Examples: Eph. 1:13
   Ye were sealed with the Holy Spirit . . . .
      Zoque: God sealed (branded) you by the Holy Spirit . . . .
Eph. 3:5 It hath now been revealed . . . .
      Zoque: Now God has made this kind of thing known . . . .

Suppose the language into which you are translating has no passive verb constructions. Write the following passages so that the passive is changed to active. If the subject is not indicated in the passage supply *someone,* or *they* underlining it to indicate that further study is needed to enable you to make the agent explicit.

Examples: Mark 1:9
   Jesus was baptized by John in the Jordan.
      John baptized Jesus in the Jordan.
Mark 1:14 John was arrested.
   Someone arrested John.

1) Mark 3:22
   He is possessed by Beelzebub.

2) Mark 2:5
   Your sins are forgiven.

3) 2 Cor. 6:12
   You are not restricted by us.

4) John 19:20
the place where Jesus was crucified

5) Col. 1:11
May you be strengthened with all power.

6) James 1:13
Let no one say . . . , "I am tempted by God."

7) Mark 2:1
It was reported that he was at home.

8) Mark 9:2
He was transfigured before them.

9) Mark 14:9
wherever the gospel is preached

10) 1 Cor. 11:31
If we judged ourselves truly, we should not be judged.

C. *Changing actives to passives.* There are some languages that have a preference for passive constructions. "Almost inevitably a Nilotic speaker will shift from the active to the passive in transitive expressions in which the agent is mentioned. The translator is obliged to do the same if he wishes his translation to be readily understood" (Nida, 1955, 57).

Change the following active constructions to passive.

Example: Acts 1:23
And they put forward two, Joseph and Matthias.
Two were put forward by them, Joseph and Matthias.

1) Mark 12:43
This poor widow has put in more than all these who are contributing.

2) John 9:13
They brought to the Pharisees the man who had formerly been blind.

3) Acts 1:6
Lord, will you at this time restore the kingdom to Israel?

4) Mark 13:5

Take heed that no one leads you astray.

5) 1 Cor. 16:10

When Timothy comes, see that you put him at ease.

D. *Causative.* "In Mark 6:16 it is impossible in many languages to translate literally Herod's words 'John, whom I beheaded,' unless one wishes to imply that Herod himself was the executioner — something which is explicitly denied later in the chapter. Accordingly, one must render this passage as 'John whom I caused to be beheaded'" (Nida, 1964, 201).

The following passages may need to be recast from active to causative action in some languages. Rewrite, making clear the relation of the actor to the action. Consult the context for names of participants and include the specific name in place of the pronoun when rewriting. The following example shows three possible ways of stating the answer.

Example: Acts 5:18

They arrested the apostles and put them in prison.

The high priest and those with him had the apostles arrested and put in prison.

The high priest and those with him caused the apostles to be arrested and put in prison.

The high priest and those with him had the soldiers arrest the apostles and put them in prison.

1) Acts 2:36

this Jesus whom you crucified.

2) Matt. 2:13

Herod is about to search for the child, to destroy him.

3) Luke 9:9

Herod said, "John I beheaded."

4) Matt. 2:16

And Herod killed all the male children in Bethlehem.

5) Matt. 14:3

For Herod had seized John and bound him and put him in prison.

6) Matt. 27:1, 2
All the chief priests and the elders bound him and led him away and delivered him to Pilate.

7) Acts 5:25
And some one came and told them, "The men whom you put in prison are standing in the temple and teaching the people."

8) Luke 22:2
The scribes were seeking how to put him to death.

9) Acts 12:1-3
About that time Herod the king laid violent hands upon some who belonged to the church. He killed James and proceeded to arrest Peter also.

10) Acts 3:15
You killed the Author of life.

SECTION 2. ABSTRACT NOUNS

"One of the significant characteristics of Indo-European languages is to express events by means of nouns (or nominalized forms), e.g., *baptism, repentance, forgiveness, sin, salvation, atonement,* etc. In many languages all of these events are predominately verbs, not nouns; and though in many instances nominal forms may be constructed, the more natural mode of expression is by means of verbal expressions. Accordingly, in many translations the renderings would make much more sense if such nouns were changed into verbs. For example, Mark 1:4 is often rendered more meaningfully and more in accordance with the grammatical requirements of the receptor language as 'John preached that the people should repent and be baptized so that God would forgive the evil which they had done' " (Nida, 1961, "New Helps for Translators," *TBT* 12/2, 52).

A. *Identifying abstract nouns.* Which noun (or nouns) in each of the following is derived from a verb and therefore has a basic semantic meaning of event or action?

Example: 1 Cor. 16:24
My love be with you all in Christ Jesus.
Answer: love

1) James 1:15
   Sin brings forth death.

2) Rom. 1:16
   for salvation to everyone who has faith

3) Rom. 3:20
   Through the law comes knowledge of sin.

4) Rev. 20:4
   Seated on them were those to whom judgment was committed.

5) 1 Thess. 2:9
   For you remember our labor and toil while we preached to you.

6) 1 Thess. 3:5
   I sent that I might know your faith, for fear that somehow the tempter had tempted you and that our labor would be in vain.

B. *Changing abstract nouns to verb phrases.* Assuming that the language into which you are translating does not have special nouns to express concepts such as those italicized in the following passages, how might you give the same meaning by using an active verb phrase for the noun? Do not use a participle.

Example: Rev. 21:4
   and *death* shall be no more
      Answer: and no one shall die any more

1) Col. 1:8
   has made known to us your *love*

2) Acts 16:13
   where we supposed there was a place of *prayer*

3) Acts 4:12
   There is *salvation* in no one else.

4) John 4:10
   If you knew the *gift* of God . . . .

5) John 3:19
   because their *deeds* were evil

6) 1 John 4:21
And this *commandment* we have from him.

7) Matt. 21:22
whatever you ask in *prayer*

8) Matt. 9:13
I came to call sinners to *repentance*. (KJV)

9) Luke 4:18
to proclaim *release* to the captives

C. *Identifying more abstract nouns.* List all of the abstract nouns that you find in the following passages. These may be derived from adjectives as well as from verbs.

Example: Rom. 6:4
We were buried therefore with him by baptism into death.
baptism, death

Eph. 1:19
and what is the immeasurable greatness of his power
greatness, power

1) Rom. 1:9
For God is my witness whom I serve.

2) Eph. 1:7, 8
In him we have redemption, the forgiveness of our trespasses, according to the riches of his grace which he lavished upon us.

3) Acts 5:31
God exalted him as Leader and Savior, to give repentance to Israel and forgiveness of sins.

4) Acts 2:42
And they devoted themselves to the apostles' teaching and fellowship, to the breaking of bread and the prayers.

5) Rom. 13:13
Let us conduct ourselves becomingly, not in reveling and drunkenness, not in debauchery and licentiousness, not in quarreling and jealousy.

D. *Changing abstract nouns to relative clauses.* Many times abstract nouns will need to be translated by relative clauses beginning with "that," "who," "which," etc. Change the abstract noun in each of the following to a relative clause. Do not use a participle.

Example: Acts 17:7
They are all acting against the *decrees* of Caesar.
They are all acting against that which Caesar has decreed.

1) Rom. 1:8
Your *faith* is proclaimed in all the world.

2) Acts 2:42
And they devoted themselves to the apostles' *teaching*.

3) Prov. 21:17
He who loves *pleasure* will be a poor man.

4) Matt. 5:9
Blessed are the *peacemakers*.

5) Rom. 1:9
For God is my *witness*, whom I serve.

E. *Review.* In the following passages, change all passive constructions to active and all italicized abstract nouns to active verb phrases, adding implicit participants as needed.

Example: 1 Pet. 1:7
at the *revelation* of Jesus Christ
at the time when Jesus Christ will reveal himself

1) Mark 2:5
Your *sins* are forgiven.

2) Matt. 28:18
All *authority* has been given to me.

3) Mark 6:14
John the *baptizer* has been raised from the dead.

4) Gal. 6:1
if a man is overtaken in any *trespass*

5) Rev. 20:4
Then I saw thrones, and seated on them were those to whom *judgment* was committed.

SECTION 3. PARTICIPLES

"Very seldom does another language even approximate the extensive use of participial attributives which occurs in the Greek or in the more literal translations into English. In no case should the translator attempt to conform the syntax artificially so as to represent this special feature of Greek" (Nida, 1947, 269).

"Grammatically all participles are adjectival; . . . but in function — that is, in respect to the kind of questions which their use answers — participles may be either adjectival or adverbial. A participle which is adjectival in function answers a question such as 'which one?' which an adjective may answer. An adverbial participle, even though it modifies a noun, answers a question which an adverb may answer, such as 'When?' 'Why?' 'How?' etc." (Greenlee, 1954, 100).

A. *Changing participles to relative clauses.* "Attributive participles may commonly be translated by relative clauses introduced by 'who' or 'which'" (Ibid., 101). Change each of the following italicized attributive participles to a relative clause, using "who," "which," or "that."

> Example: John 6:51
> *I am the living bread.*
> I am the bread that gives life.

> 1) James 1:11
> the sun rises with its *scorching heat*

> 2) 2 Cor. 6:16
> For we are the temple of the *living God*

> 3) Jude 13
> *wandering stars* for whom the nether gloom of darkness has been reserved

> 4) John 4:10
> He would have given you *living water.*

> 5) Isa. 30:28
> His breath is like an *overflowing stream.*

> 6) Dan. 3:6
> came near to the door of the *burning fiery furnace*

7) Rom. 2:15
And their *conflicting thoughts* accuse or perhaps excuse them.

B. *Changing participles to finite verbs.* Assume that the language into which you are translating has no participles. Rewrite the following passages, using a finite verb form. You may need to make more than one sentence in order to do this. Add any implicit participants as needed.

Example: John 16:1
I have said all this to you to keep you from *falling away*.
I have said all this so you will not fall away.

1) John 5:18
also called God his Father, *making* himself equal with God.

2) Acts 2:13
But others *mocking* said, "They are filled with new wine."

3) Mark 15:29
And those who passed by derided him, *wagging* their heads, and *saying* , . . .

4) Mark 6:20
Herod feared John, *knowing* that he was a righteous and holy man.

5) Acts 5:7
His wife came in, not *knowing* what had happened.

6) Acts 7:56
I see the heavens opened, and the Son of man *standing* at the right hand of God.

C. *Changing finite verbs to participles.* In Aguaruna, of Peru, the participle is used frequently, often in preference to a series of finite verbs, i.e., several English clauses connected by "and" may be one Aguaruna sentence with participial phrases and one finite verb.

Example: Mark 8:23
And he took the blind man by the hand and led him out of the village; and when he had spit on his eyes and laid his hands upon him, he asked him, "Do you see anything?"
Aguaruna: Taking the blind man by the hand, leading

him out of the village, spitting on his eyes, laying his hands upon him, speaking to him, he asked, "Do you see anything?"

Rewrite the following so that they consist of one sentence made up of participial phrases and one main verb. Do not change the direct quotes, but keep them as separate sentences. Sometimes a compound verb phrase may be needed, such as "having seen."

1) Mark 11:4
And they went away, and found a colt tied at the door out in the open street; and they untied it.

2) John 9:25
Though I was blind, now I see.

3) John 1:43
The next day Jesus decided to go to Galilee. And he found Philip and said to him, "Follow me."

4) Mark 8:6
And he commanded the crowd to sit down, and he took the seven loaves, and having given thanks he broke them and gave them to the disciples to set before the people.

5) Mark 10:16
And he took them in his arms and blessed them, laying his hands upon them.

6) 1 Cor. 11:29
For anyone who eats and drinks without discerning the body eats and drinks judgment upon himself.

D. *Review.* For each of the following passages rewrite eliminating abstract nouns and participles by using an active verb, non-participial expression.

Example: John 4:10
He would have given you *living* water.
He would give you water which will cause you to live.

1) Acts 15:16
I will rebuild the *dwelling* of David.

2) 1 Cor. 7:19
For neither *circumcision* counts for anything nor *uncircumcision,* but *keeping* the *commandments* of God.

3) Rom. 13:10
Therefore *love* is the *fulfilling* of the law.

4) Rom. 13:6
For the authorities are *ministers* of God, *attending* to this very thing.

5) Rom. 12:7
he who teaches, in his *teaching*

SECTION 4. ATTRIBUTIVES

"Some adjectives in the Greek or English do not correspond to any adjectives in the aboriginal language. "Faithless generation" must be changed in Eastern Aztec to 'people who do not believe.' 'False Christs' must be changed to 'Christs who really are not' " (Nida, 1947, 269).

A. *Changing attributives.* There are some languages in which nouns are not modified by adjectives in the same way as in English. In some cases a relative clause, a conditional clause, a verb phrase, or some other adjustment may be used. Note the following examples of possible rewording. Then reconstruct the italicized part of the following passages to eliminate the adjective. Be sure the English still gives the right sense after your change.

Example: 2 Cor. 1:12
not by *earthly wisdom*
wisdom that is derived from those of this earth
wisdom that people possess

1) James 1:19
know this, my *beloved brethren*

2) Rev. 11:7
that ascends from the *bottomless pit*

3) 1 Pet. 3:5
the *holy women* who hoped in God

4) Heb. 12:23
and to the spirits of *just men* made perfect

5) 1 Pet. 2:15
the ignorance of *foolish men*

6) 1 Tim. 4:8
bodily training is of some value

7) Prov. 22:24
nor go with a *wrathful man*

8) John 6:57
as the *living Father* sent me

9) 1 Pet. 2:9
but you are a *chosen race*

10) Prov. 21:9
than in a house with a *contentious woman*

11) Isa. 35:4
say to those who are of a *fearful heart*

12) 2 Tim. 3:8
men of *corrupt minds*

13) Acts 4:13
they were *uneducated men*

14) Acts 4:6
all who were of the *high-priestly family*

15) Rom. 2:5
By your *impenitent heart* you are storing up wrath for yourself.

B. *Review.* As you rewrite the following to eliminate the adjectival construction, also change the abstract noun that it modifies to a verb phrase.

Example: Luke 1:72
and to remember his *holy covenant*
    Amuzgo: that word which he arranged which was clean

1) 2 Cor. 7:10
For *godly grief* produces a repentance . . . .

2) Eph. 5:4
Let there be no filthiness, nor *silly talk* . . . .

3) 2 Tim. 1:9
who saved us and called us with a *holy calling*

4) 2 Tim. 3:8
and *counterfeit faith*

5) Heb. 7:16
   but by the power of an *indestructible life*

6) Heb. 10:27
   but a *fearful prospect* of judgment

SECTION 5. OBJECTIVIZATION AND PERSONIFICATION

A. *Objectivization.* In each of the following, the italicized word, which is an abstract noun, is being used as if it referred to an object rather than an event or abstraction. Rewrite the passage eliminating the objectivization.

Example: Luke 1:12
   Fear fell upon him (Zechariah).
   Zechariah became afraid.

1) Mark 5:34
   Your *faith* has made you well.

2) James 1:20
   The *anger* of man does not work the righteousness of God.

3) Rom. 13:10
   Love does no wrong to a neighbor.

4) Acts 2:43
   and *fear* came upon every soul

5) Rom. 5:5
   God's *love* has been poured into our hearts.

6) Phil. 1:9
   It is my prayer that your *love* may abound more and more.

7) Luke 1:79
   to guide our feet into the way of *peace*

8) 1 John 1:4
   We are writing this that our *joy* may be complete.

B. *Personification.* "When abstract nouns are associated with other forms which imply personality, then these nouns tend to *personify* the Events or the Abstractions which they represent" (Beekman-Callow, 1974, 221).

Each of the following involves a personification. Suggest a possible rewording eliminating the personification.

Example: 1 Cor. 15:55
O death, where is thy victory?
O grave, where is thy sting?
Nothing will at that time cause people to die.
People will never die again.

1) Rom. 6:12
Let not sin therefore reign in your mortal bodies.

2) 1 John 4:18
Perfect love casts out fear.

3) Rom. 11:11
Through their transgression salvation has come to the Gentiles.

4) Rom. 13:1
Salvation is nearer to us now than when we first believed.

5) Rev. 12:12
Rejoice then, O heavens and you that dwell therein!

6) Matt. 2:6
And you, O Bethlehem, in the land of Judah, are by no means least among the rulers of Judah.

7) Mark 4:39
And he said to the sea, "Peace! Be still!"

8) Luke 13:34
O Jerusalem, Jerusalem, How often would I have gathered your children together. . . !

9) Mark 11:14
May no one ever eat fruit from you again.

SECTION 6. CHRONOLOGICAL ORDER

In some languages it is essential to relate events in the sequence in which they occurred. What adjustment in ordering might be necessary in the translation of the following passages?

Example: Mark 7:17
And when he entered the house, and left the people, his disciples asked him about the parable.
And when he had left the people, he entered the house . . . .

1) John 4:39
2) Acts 5:30, 31
3) Rev. 7:9
4) Rom. 4:18
5) John 1:32, 33
6) John 12:39-41
7) Rom. 6:3
8) 1 Cor. 15:24-26
9) John 4:1, 2

SECTION 7. NEGATIVES

Languages handle negatives in many different ways. A negative in the source language will not always be translated by a negative in the receptor language.

A. *Double negatives* may need to be translated by a positive statement in some languages. Restate the following, eliminating the negatives.

Example: John 1:3
Without him was *not* anything made that was made.
   Chinanteco: All things came into being because that person made all that exists.

1) Luke 18:29, 30
There is *no* man who has left house or wife or brothers or parents or children, for the sake of the kingdom of God who will *not* receive manifold more.

2) Matt. 10:29
And *not* one of them will fall to the ground *without* your Father's will.

3) Matt. 10:38
And he who does *not* take his cross and follow me is *not* worthy of me.

4) 1 Cor. 9:21
not being *without* the law.

5) Mark 4:34
He did *not* speak to them *without* a parable.

B. *Restating as a positive statement.* Other negatives occur with words such as "till," "until," and "except." These may sometimes need to be translated with a positive statement. Restate the following, using a positive statement rather than a negative one to convey the same meaning.

> Example: Mark 4:22
> > For there is *nothing* hid, *except* to be made manifest!
> > Cuicateco: Everything that is hidden will have to be exhibited (shown).

1) John 13:38
The cock will *not* crow, *till* you have denied me three times.

2) John 13:10
does *not* need to wash, *except* for his feet

3) John 20:25
Unless I see in his hands the print of the nails I will *not* believe.

4) Luke 13:35
You will *not* see me *until* you say . . . .

5) Matt. 13:57
A prophet is *not without* honor *except* in his own country.

6) Luke 21:32
This generation will *not* pass away *till* all has taken place.

C. *Placement of the negative.* In some languages an adjustment has to be made by placing the negative with the verb rather than with the noun or pronoun. Change the following so that the negative goes with the verb.

> Example: John 14:6
> > No one comes to the Father, but by me.
> > A person does not come to the Father but by me.

1) Rom. 13:8
Owe *no one* anything, except to love one another.

2) 1 Cor. 1:14
I baptized *none of you* except Crispus and Gaius.

3) Mark 6:5
And he could do *no mighty work* there, except that he laid his hands upon a few sick.

4) John 19:15
We have *no king* but Caesar.

5) Mark 6:8
He charged them to take *nothing* for their journey except a staff.

D. *Changing negative to "only" clauses.* In some languages the negatives are eliminated in certain constructions and *only* is used to carry the meaning. Change the following by using *only* and eliminating the negative.

Example: Matt. 5:13
It is *no longer* good for anything *except* to be thrown out.
It is now good *only* to be thrown out.

1) Matt. 18:3
Unless you turn and become like children, you will *never* enter the kingdom of heaven.

2) Matt. 5:26
You will *never* get out till you have paid the last penny.

3) Matt. 17:21
But this kind *never* comes out *except* by prayer and fasting.

4) Rev. 14:3
No one could learn that song *except* the hundred and forty-four thousand who had been redeemed from the earth.

5) John 3:3
Unless one is born anew, he *cannot* see the kingdom of God.

6) Gen. 44:23
Unless your youngest brother comes down with you, you shall see my face *no* more.

SECTION 8. REVIEW

A. *Identifying adjustments.* What adjustment has been made in each of the following, probably because of the obligatory categories of the receptor language? Choose the correct letter from the following to match your answer. There may be other adjustments also, but look for ones listed here.

a) honorifics
b) dual person

c) obligatory possession
d) different use of negatives
e) extended use of plural for singular
f) extended use of singular for plural
g) extended use of person
h) different tense system
i) different aspect system
j) obligatory "dead" suffix

1) John 4:12
   Are you greater than our father Jacob?
      Amuesha: Do you surpass how he used to rule, our dead grandfather Jacob?

2) John 3:2
   Rabbi, we know that you are a teacher come from God.
      Aguaruna: Teacher, I know saying, "Surely he is one who teaches what God has said."

3) John 3:21
   he who does what is true
      Chinanteco: all those who are engaged in right.

4) 1 Tim. 1:1
   Paul, an apostle of Christ Jesus . . . .
      Aguaruna: I am me, I am Paul. I am one chosen by Jesus Christ.

5) Luke 9:37
   when they had come down from the mountain
      Balinese: when he (very important one) came down from the mountain followed by his disciples

6) Col. 4:9
   and with him Onesimus, the faithful and beloved brother
      Aguaruna: Tychicus is coming with our beloved brother, Onesimus, who is an obeyer of Christ, with that one

7) Acts 7:20
   At this time Moses was born, and was beautiful before God.
      Aguaruna: When they stayed like that one little child was born-remote-past, one-chosen by God, who was to be our grandfather Moses.

8) John 1:3

Without him was not anything made that was made.

Chinanteco: All things came into being because that person made all things that exist.

9) Mark 5:27

She had heard the reports about Jesus.

Aguaruna: She had heard-repeatedly people saying, "Jesus truly heals many."

10) Acts 16:24

He put them into the inner prison.

Pame: He took them-two into the room farthest inside the jail.

B. *Identifying adjustments, continued.* Study the translation made of each of the following passages. What adjustment was made? Identify and label each adjustment.

Example: John 4:1

the Pharisees had heard

Tepehua: the Pharisees had heard that it was said

Implicit information made explicit.

1) John 4:5

near the field that Jacob gave to his son Joseph

Tepehua: It was near the land of the ancient Israelite who was called Jacob. There was where he gave it as a gift to his son who was called Joseph.

2) John 4:12

Are you greater than our father Jacob, who gave us the well?

Campa: Do you surpass our forefather dead Jacob who made this well for us?

3) John 4:12

and drank from it himself, and his sons, and his cattle

Aguaruna: He was one who drank this water, his children also drank it, and he also gave his domesticated animals to drink from it.

4) John 4:15

The woman said to him, "Sir, give me this water, that I may not thirst, nor come here to draw."

Chol: The woman said to Jesus, "Teacher, give me this water in order that I will not have to continually have thirst; in order that I will not continually come to draw water here," she said.

5) John 4:29

"Come, see a man who told me all that I ever did. Can this be the Christ?"

Northern Totonaco: Go see a man who told me all that I have done. Perhaps he is the Christ.

6) John 4:31

Meanwhile the disciples besought him, saying, "Rabbi, eat."

Chinanteco: In the meantime, the disciples were saying to Jesus, "Teacher, eat."

7) John 4:45

having seen all that he had done in Jerusalem at the feast

Tepehua: since they had seen all the miracles that he had done in the town of Jerusalem when there was a fiesta there

8) John 4:50

Jesus said to him, "Go; your son will live."

Aguaruna: He said to him, "Return, your son will not die."

9) John 4:52

So he asked them the hour when he began to mend, and they said to him, "Yesterday at the seventh hour the fever left him."

Aguaruna: When they said this he asked, "Where was the sun when he recovered?" When he said it they said, "Yesterday when the sun leaned the fever cooled."

10) John 4:53

The father knew that was the hour when Jesus had said to him, "Your son will live"; and he himself believed, and all his household.

Tepehua: Well, the father of the sick one immediately understood that that was the hour when Jesus said that. Well, that man and all that were in his house immediately believed in Jesus.

CHAPTER 15

Rhetorical Questions

TEXT: Beekman-Callow, 1974, chapter 15

ADDITIONAL READING:

Andrews, Henrietta, 1972, "Rhetorical Questions in Otomi of the State of Mexico," *NOT* 44:25-8

Beekman, John, 1972, "Analyzing and Translating the Questions of the New Testament," *NOT* 44:3-21

Cowan, Marion M., 1960, "The Translation of Questions into Huixteco," *TBT* 11/3, 123-25

Crouch, Marjorie, 1972, "Rhetorical Questions in Bagla of Ghana," *NOT* 44:32-36

Elkins, Richard E., 1972, "Supposition Rules for Rhetorical Questions in English and Western Bukidnon Manobo," *NOT* 44:21-24

Kirkpatrick, Lilla, 1972, "Rhetorical Questions in Korku of Central India," *NOT* 44:28-32

Levinsohn, Stephen, 1972, "Questions in Inga of Colombia and Their Use in Mark's Gospel," *NOT* 44:36-39

Longacre, R. E., 1972, "Rhetorical Questions in Trique," *NOT* 44:39, 40

Nida, 1964, 209

A. *Real versus rhetorical questions.* The real question is used to elicit information; the rhetorical question is used to convey or call attention to information. In each of the following passages there is a question asked. Which ones are real questions and which ones are rhetorical questions? Consult the context if necessary.

Examples: Mark 8:37
　For what can a man give in return for his life?
　　Rhetorical question
Matt. 13:10
　Why do you speak to them in parables?
　　Real question

1) Heb. 12:7
God is treating you as sons; for what son is there whom his father does not discipline?

2) 1 Tim. 3:5
For if a man does not know how to manage his own household, how can he care for God's church?

3) Mark 4:38
They woke him and said to him, "Teacher, do you not care if we perish?"

4) Gal. 4:16
Have I then become your enemy by telling you the truth?

5) Matt. 9:14
Then the disciples of John came to him, saying, "Why do we and the Pharisees fast, but your disciples do not fast?"

6) Acts 2:7, 8
And they were amazed and wondered, saying, "Are not all these who are speaking Galileans? And how is it that we hear . . . ?"

7) John 9:17
So they again said to the blind man, "What do you say about him, since he has opened your eyes?"

8) John 6:70
Jesus answered them, "Did I not choose you, the twelve, and one of you is a devil?"

B. *Changing rhetorical questions to statements.* "Rhetorical questions where the answer seems obvious to us, leave the Huixtecos confused as to the answer, so these were changed into statements to provide the correct answer for them, as in Matt. 7:9-11 , . . . 'If he (your son) asks you for fish to eat, not a snake you would give him. You whose hearts are not good, know what good gifts you will give your children. Your father in heaven surpassingly knows what good gifts he will give to those who ask him.'

"The Huixteco brethren did not like the question in John 8:46 'Which of you convicts me of sin?' because it indicated to them that Christ had sinned but that no one there had found it out yet. So this question was changed to the emphatic statement, 'You cannot find *my* sin'" (Cowan, 1960, 125).

Change the following questions to statements that will convey the meaning of the rhetorical question. You will need to change the positive question to a negative statement.

Example: John 18:35
Pilate said, "Am I a Jew?"
Pilate said, "I'm not a Jew."

1) Matt. 5:13
If salt has lost its taste, how shall its saltness be restored?

2) Matt. 5:46
For if you love those who love you, what reward have you?

3) Rom. 3:9
Are we Jews any better off?

4) Rom. 6:15
Are we to sin because we are not under the law but under grace?

5) Heb. 1:5
For to what angel did God ever say, "Thou art my Son ..."?

C. *Changing rhetorical questions with a negative particle to positive statements.* Many times rhetorical questions are asked in a negative construction. As you change the following questions to statements, change to a positive construction as well.

Example: John 7:19
Did not Moses give you the law?
Moses gave you the law.

1) Matt. 5:46
Do not even the tax collectors do the same?

2) Matt. 12:5
Or have you not read in the law how on the sabbath the priests in the temple profane the sabbath, and are guiltless?

3) Matt. 13:55

Is not this the carpenter's son? Is not his mother called Mary?

4) John 4:35

Do you not say, "There are four months, then comes the harvest"?

5) Acts 5:4

While it remained unsold, did it not remain your own? And after it was sold, was it not at your disposal?

D. *Real versus rhetorical questions continued.* In the following passages, change all rhetorical questions to statements. Real questions should be left as questions. See examples in A, B, and C, above.

1) John 6:30

So they said to him, "Then what sign do you do, that we may see, and believe you?"

2) Matt. 11:3

. . . and said to him, "Are you he who is to come or shall we look for another?"

3) 2 Cor. 1:17

Was I vacillating when I wanted to do this? Do I make plans like a worldly man, ready to say Yes and No at once?

4) 2 Cor. 2:15, 16

For we are the aroma of Christ to God among those who are being saved and among those who are perishing. Who is sufficient for these things?

5) Matt. 7:9

Or what man of you, if his son asks him for a loaf, will give him a stone?

6) Heb. 2:3

How shall we escape if we neglect so great salvation?

7) 1 Cor. 2:16

For who has known the mind of the Lord so as to instruct him?

8) 1 Cor. 4:7

For who sees anything different in you? What have you that you did not receive? If you then received it, why do you boast as if it were not a gift?

9) John 7:45-52

(entire passage — questions for information should be kept as questions.)

E. *Supplying the answer to a rhetorical question.* Assume you are translating into a language in which the following may be translated by a rhetorical question but in which the answer to the question must be given. Give the answer for the question in each of the following passages.

Example: Romans 8:31

If God is for us, who is against us?

No one can be against us.

1) Luke 5:21

Who can forgive sins but God only?

2) John 14:2

If it were not so, would I have told you that I go to prepare a place for you?

3) 2 Cor. 6:15

Or what has a believer in common with an unbeliever?

4) John 8:57

You are not yet fifty years old, and have you seen Abraham?

5) Rom. 8:24

For in this hope we were saved . . . . Who hopes for what he sees?

6) John 6:9

There is a lad here who has five barley loaves and two fish; but what are they among so many?

7) 1 Cor. 2:11

For what person knows a man's thoughts except the spirit of the man which is in him?

8) Heb. 13:6

The Lord is my helper, I will not be afraid; what can man do to me?

F. *Functions of rhetorical questions.* Rhetorical questions have different functions. After studying the passage given in its context, decide which of the following functions applies to the passage. Answer with the correct letter from the following list. Some may have more than one possible answer.

a) to emphasize the negative or affirmative aspect of a statement

b) to make a statement of incertitude, contingency, doubt, or deliberation

c) to make an evaluation or appraisive statement, usually accompanied with favorable or unfavorable emotional attitudes supplied by the context

d) to make a command (entreaty, exhortation, or injunction)

e) to introduce a new subject or new aspect of the same subject.

Example: Matt. 8:26

Why are you afraid, O men of little faith?

c or d

1) Luke 13:20

And again he said, "To what shall I compare the kingdom of God?"

2) Luke 19:23

Why then did you not put my money into the bank, and at my coming I should have collected it with interest?

3) Luke 12:6

Are not five sparrows sold for two pennies?

4) Luke 12:14

But he said to him, "Man, who made me a judge or divider over you?"

5) John 4:29

Come, see a man who told me all that I ever did. Can this be the Christ?

6) Rom. 14:10

Why do you pass judgment on your brother?

7) Mark 14:6

But Jesus said, "Why do you trouble her?"

8) Matt. 7:3

Why do you see the speck that is in your brother's eye, but do not notice the log that is in your own eye?

G. *Review.* In each of the following rhetorical questions there is an additional potential translation adjustment. (1) State what this potential adjustment is and (2) change the rhetorical question into a statement, adjusting the item identified in number 1.

Example: Col. 2:20

If with Christ you died to the elemental spirits of the universe, why do you live as if you still belonged to the world?

1) conditional clause
2) With Christ you died to the elemental spirits of the universe, therefore don't live as if you still belonged to the world.

1) Mark 1:24

and he cried out, "What have you to do with us, Jesus of Nazareth?"

2) Mark 8:4

And his disciples answered him, "How can one feed these men with bread here in the desert?"

3) Mark 8:36

For what does it profit a man, to gain the whole world and forfeit his life?

4) Mark 12:26

And as for the dead being raised, have you not read in the book of Moses, in the passage about the bush, how God said to him . . . ?

5) John 5:47

But if you do not believe his writings, how will you believe my words?

6) Luke 8:25
He said to them, "Where is your faith?"

7) Luke 18:7
And will not God vindicate his elect . . . ?

8) Rev. 6:17
The great day of their wrath has come, and who can stand before it?

9) John 8:53
Are you greater than our father Abraham, who died?

10) John 11:40
Jesus said to her, "Did I not tell you that if you would believe you would see the glory of God?"

H. *Review.* For each of the following passages look for two adjustments that might need to be made in translation and identify the item you are referring to. These will include passive constructions, abstract nouns, genitive constructions, participles, certain attributives, negatives, and obligatory possession.

Example: Acts 15:7
And after there had been much debate, Peter rose and said to them, "Brethren, you know that . . . ."

debate — abstract noun
brethren — obligatory possession

1) Acts 3:19
Repent therefore, and turn again, that your sins may be blotted out, that times of refreshing may come from the presence of the Lord.

2) Acts 6:4
But we will devote ourselves to prayer and to the ministry of the word.

3) Acts 7:55
gazed into heaven and saw the glory of God, and Jesus standing at the right hand of God

4) Acts 7:60
And he knelt down and cried with a loud voice, "Lord, do not hold this sin against them."

5) Acts 8:1

And Saul was consenting to his death. And on that day a great persecution arose against the church.

6) Acts 9:1

But Saul, still breathing threats and murder against the disciples of the Lord, went to the high priest.

7) Acts 10:23

So he called them in to be his guests. The next day he arose and went off with them, and some of the brethren from Joppa accompanied him.

8) Acts 10:33

So I sent to you at once, and you have been kind enough to come. Now therefore we are all here present in the sight of God, to hear all that you have been commanded by the Lord.

9) Acts 14:8

Now at Lystra there was a man sitting, who could not use his feet; he was a cripple from birth, who had never walked.

10) Acts 22:1

Brethren and fathers, hear the defense which I now make before you.

I. *Identifying translation adjustments.* The following passage is a back-translation of John 2:1-11 in the Ojitlan Chinantec language of Mexico. Compare this with the RSV or ASV and see how many adjustments you can find that were made in this translation. List the adjustments and label those you can identify. For example, to the phrase *at Cana*, a classifier, *town*, is added.

¹On the third day they made a wedding feast in the town of Cana which pertains to Galilee. The mother of Jesus was standing there. ²And they called Jesus and his learners to the wedding feast. ³The wine ran out. So the mother of Jesus spoke. She told Jesus, "They have no more wine." ⁴So Jesus told his mother, "Wait, woman. I know what I am going to do about it. For my hour has not yet come." ⁵So his mother said, speaking to all the servants, "Do everything he says." ⁶Six large waterpots were standing there, where they put water which they said was for purifying according to the law of the

Jews. Each pot held about eight small waterpots. [7]So Jesus told those servants, "Fill up those large waterpots." And they filled them. [8]After this, Jesus said, "Dip up a little of that and go and show it to the chief elder in charge of the wedding feast." So they went with it. [9]So that elder extracted the truth about the quality of the wine that had been just plain water. And he was unaware of the origin of the wine. But the servants who poured the water into the pots knew where it came from. So the elder called the groom. [10]And he told him, "All other men give first the good wine. And when they have drunk and become satisfied, they give them wine that is less than the best. But right now you have given us wine far superior to that which ran out before." [11]There first did Jesus a miracle in the town of Cana in the land of Galilee. So that the people saw how big he was. Having seen this his learners, more than ever they believed in Him.

CHAPTER 16

Genitive Constructions

TEXT: Beekman-Callow, 1974, chapter 16

ADDITIONAL READING:

Frantz, Chester I., 1965, "Genitives" (In Beekman, John, 1965, *NOT with Drills*), 200-14

Greenlee, J. Harold, 1950, "The Genitive Case in the New Testament," *TBT* 1/2, 68-70

Marshall, A., 1952, "The Genitive of Quality in the New Testament," *TBT* 3/1, 14-16

Nida, Eugene A., 1950, "Equivalents of the Genitive in Other Languages," *TBT* 1/2, 70-72

Nida, 1964, 64-66

Nida and Taber, 1969, 35-41

Taylor, John M., 1965, "Notes on the Greek Genitive" (In Beekman, John, 1965, *NOT with Drills*), 194-200

Wonderly, William L., 1953, "Information-Correspondence and the Translation of Ephesians into Zoque," *TBT* 4/1, 15-18

SECTION 1. RESTATING GENITIVE CONSTRUCTIONS

A. *Genitive constructions restated as State propositions.* "Certain genitive constructions may be restated in the form of a State proposition. When this is the case, the two nominals usually represent Things, though there is a less common form in which an Abstraction and a Thing are represented" (Beekman-Callow, 1974, 251).

Restate each of the following as a State proposition, eliminating the genitive construction.

Example: Mark 14:13
  jar of water
    the jar contains water

147

1) Eph. 1:13
   the word of truth

2) Mark 1:9
   Nazareth of Galilee

3) Mark 14:3
   the house of Simon

4) Rom. 11:22
   the kindness of God

5) Eph. 1:7
   the riches of his grace

6) Matt. 26:71
   Jesus of Nazareth

7) Acts 11:5
   the city of Joppa

8) Mark 6:15
   prophets of old

B. *Genitive constructions restated as Event propositions.* "Event propositions, represented by a genitive construction, consist of an Event linked by different relations to Things or Abstractions" (Beekman-Callow, 1974, 257).

In the following, one of the nominals in the genitive construction is an abstract noun representing an Event semantically. Rewrite without using an abstract noun or a genitive construction.

Example: Eph. 1:1
   by the will of God
      as God willed (as God wanted)

Titus 1:1
   Paul, a servant of God
      I, Paul, serve God

1) 1 Peter 1:11
   the sufferings of Christ

2) John 6:29
   the work of God

3) Col. 1:10
   the knowledge of God

4) Luke 1:41
the greeting of Mary

5) Luke 24:49
the promise of my Father

6) 1 Cor. 2:1
the testimony of God

7) John 3:36
the wrath of God

8) Col. 1:7
minister of Christ

9) 1 Tim. 6:10
the love of money

10) Gal. 1:10
the favor of men

C. *Genitive constructions containing abstract nouns.* In the following genitive constructions the word following the *of* is an abstract noun. Change this noun to a verb phrase and eliminate the genitive construction by using a relative clause. Add any participants as needed.

Example: Heb. 11:9
the land of promise
the land which God had promised him

1) Rom. 14:9
Lord both of the dead and of the living

2) 2 Cor. 1:3
God of all comfort

3) 2 Cor. 13:11
God of love

4) Mal. 2:17
the God of judgment

5) Heb. 7:2
king of righteousness

D. *Genitive construction containing implied Events.* In some genitive constructions the Event is only implied and has to be supplied from the context. Reword the following eliminating the genitive construction by making the implied Event explicit.

Example: Luke 2:11
    the city of David
        the city where David had been born

1) Matt. 3:4
    garment of camel's hair

2) Luke 4:17
    the book of the prophet Isaiah

3) Luke 1:10
    the hour of incense

4) John 1:29
    the Lamb of God

5) Luke 3:2
    the word of God

6) Luke 2:41
    the feast of the Passover

7) Matt. 12:8
    the lord of the sabbath

8) 2 Cor. 3:3
    tables of stone

E. *Genitive construction representing two propositions.* When two Events or an Event and an Abstraction are involved in a genitive construction, it is necessary to elucidate not only the propositions themselves but also the relation between them. Rewrite each of the following, eliminating the genitive construction, restating it as two propositions, and showing the relation between the two resultant propositions.

Example: John 5:29
    the resurrection of life
        (people) will rise *and then* (they) will live

1) Heb. 2:15
    fear of death

2) Heb. 10:22
    assurance of faith

3) Eph. 1:5
   the purpose of his will

4) Eph. 1:7
   the forgiveness of our trespasses

5) Eph. 2:12
   the covenants of promise

6) Eph. 3:6
   partakers of the promise

7) Eph. 3:12
   confidence of access

8) Eph. 4:13
   unity of the faith

9) Col. 1:9
   the knowledge of his will

F. *Genitive constructions using ". . . of God."* In each of the
following genitive constructions the word *God* occurs following
of. Rewrite so as to make clear the relationship between the first
word of the construction and *God,* but without using a preposi-
tion or possessive construction. You may need to study the context.

Example: Eph. 1:1
   by the will of God
      as God willed (as God wanted)
Titus 1:1
   Paul, a servant of God
      I, Paul, serve God

1) Col. 1:25
   to make the *word of God* fully known

2) 2 Thess. 1:5
   This is evidence of the righteous *judgment of God,* that
   you may be made worthy of the *kingdom of God,* for which
   you are suffering

3) 1 Tim. 1:1
   Paul, an apostle of Christ Jesus by *command of God*

4) 1 Tim. 6:11
   But as for you, *man of God,* shun all this.

5) 2 Tim. 1:8
but take your share of suffering for the gospel in the *power of God*

6) 2 Tim. 3:4
lovers of pleasure rather than *lovers of God*

7) Titus 2:10
so that in everything they may adorn the *doctrine of God* our Savior

8) Heb. 4:9
there remains a sabbath rest for the *people of God*

9) Heb. 9:24
now to appear in the *presence of God* on our behalf

G. *Making the implied Event explicit.* The following phrases indicating possession, without using *of*, cannot be translated into some languages with a simple possession. Make explicit the verb that tells the relationship.

Example: Prov. 10:15
a rich man's wealth
the wealth a rich man possesses

1) John 4:6
Jacob's well

2) Mark 2:8
John's disciples

3) 1 John 1:10
his word

4) 1 John 2:12
your sins

5) Col. 1:24
Christ's afflictions

6) Mark 3:27
strong man's house

7) Mark 1:39
their synagogues

8) Acts 16:26
every one's fetters

9) Acts 21:11
he took Paul's girdle

10) 2 Cor. 2:17
God's word

H. *Changing genitive constructions.* In the following various kinds of genitive constructions occur. Rewrite each of them, making the full meaning clear. Express Event ideas by verbs.

Example: James 1:1
servant of God
a person who serves God

1) 2 Tim. 3:4
lovers of pleasure rather than lovers of God

2) Phil. 1:3
in all my remembrance of you

3) Matt. 8:26
men of little faith

4) Acts 11:5
city of Joppa

5) Col. 1:20
the blood of his cross

6) Acts 1:19
inhabitants of Jerusalem

7) Acts 13:12
the teaching of the Lord

8) James 5:15
the prayer of faith

9) Eph. 6:16
the shield of faith

Section 2. Classifying Genitive Constructions

A. *Those that may be restated as State propositions.* For the purpose of classification, the nominal which is not in the genitive case is labeled a, and the one which is, is labeled b. The typical genitive construction is thus "a of b," where "of" is used to represent the genitive case. Classify the passages given below according to these classifications, and restate as state propositions.

a) POSSESSION — A is possessed by B
b) PART-WHOLE — A is part of B, the whole
c) DEGREE — A indicates the degree of B
d) KINSHIP — A and B are related by kinship
e) ROLE — A and B are related by role
f) LOCATION — A is located in B
g) IDENTIFICATION — A is identified by B
h) CONTENT — A contains B
i) MEASUREMENT — A measures B
j) REFERENCE — A is about B
k) SUBSTANCE — A consists of B

1) Mark 14:3
   jar of ointment

2) Luke 1:26
   a city of Galilee

3) Luke 2:4
   the city of Nazareth

4) Mark 2:18
   John's disciples

5) Mark 3:27
   the strong man's house

6) 2 Kings 7:1
   a measure of fine meal

7) Matt. 10:2
   son of Zebedee

8) John 19:40
   the body of Jesus

9) Rom. 9:32
   the riches of his glory

10) John 19:2
    crown of thorns

B. *Those that may be restated as Event propositions.* In the following the Event is explicit. Classify the passages given below according to these classifications, and restate as Event propositions.

a) AGENT — B does A
b) EXPERIENCER — A happens to B

c) REGARD — A is done with regard to B
d) CONTENT — B is the content of A
e) TIME — one indicates the time of the other
f) MANNER — one describes how the other took place
g) DEGREE — A indicates the degree of B

Example: Acts 1:22
   the baptism of John
      AGENT — John baptized people

1) Rev. 15:3
   the song of Moses

2) Rev. 2:15
   the teaching of the Nicolaitans

3) Rom. 2:5
   day of wrath and revelation

4) Acts 10:45
   the gift of the Holy Spirit

5) Luke 3:6
   the salvation of God

6) Eph. 1:17
   knowledge of him

7) Rom. 3:18
   fear of God

8) Heb. 1:3
   word of his power

9) Rom. 3:20
   knowledge of sin

10) John 5:42
   love of God

C. *Those in which the Event is implicit and which may be restated as Event propositions.* In the following the Event is implicit. Classify the passages given below according to these classifications, and restate as Event propositions.

  a) GOAL — B does the implicit Event to A
  b) MANNER — B does the implicit Event in the manner A

c) MANNER — the implicit Event is done in the manner A with
   regard to B

d) TIME — B does the implicit Event at the time A

e) RECIPIENT — the implicit Event is done to the thing A, and B
   is the recipient of A

f) AGENT — one causes the state represented by the other

Example: Matt. 2:1
   in the days of Herod the king
      TIME — when Herod the king was ruling

1) Col. 3:15
   peace of Christ

2) Acts 7:45
   the days of David

3) John 2:17
   zeal of thine house (KJV)

4) Heb. 5:7
   days of his flesh

SECTION 3. REVIEW

The following passage is a back-translation into English from
Aguaruna, Peru, of Colossians 1:1-4. Compare this with the RSV
and see how many adjustments you can find. Label these adjustments by quoting the words from RSV and stating the name of the
adjustments. For example, you might write, "abstract noun
changed to verb phrase," "genitive construction changed to verb
phrase," etc. There will be some adjustments that you have not
yet studied, but note and label as many of these as you can.

Colossians 1:1-4

¹It's me. I am Paul. I am one sent by Jesus Christ, because
God said 'do thus.' Timothy, Jesus' follower, he also is with
me. ²I with him writing paper, that (paper) I send to you all,
you who live in Colossae, you being those who say 'truly God
lives,' you being those who follow Jesus Christ. May God, our
father, being merciful to you give you all peaceful life.

³Jesus Christ is our big-one (Lord). Asking his father, God,
I thank him (God), ⁴because I heard that you believe in
Jesus Christ, and I heard that you love (mutually) those who
follow Jesus Christ . . . .

CHAPTER 17

Propositions and Semantic Structures

TEXT: Beekman-Callow, 1974, chapter 17

ADDITIONAL READING:

Beekman, John, 1970, "A Structural Display of Propositions in Jude," *NOT* 37:27-31

Beekman, John, 1970, "Propositions and their Relations within Discourse," *NOT* 37:6-23

Blight, Richard C., 1970, "An Alternate Display of Jude," *NOT* 37:32-36

Callow, Kathleen, 1970, "More on Propositions and their Relations within a Discourse," *NOT* 37:23-27

Deibler, Ellis W., "Translating from Basic Structure," *TBT* 19/1, 14-16

Deibler, Ellis W., 1969, "Basic Structure of 1 Corinthians," *NOT* 31:34-39

Frantz, Donald G., 1968, "Translation and Underlying Structure I: Relations," *NOT* 30:22-28

Frantz, Donald G., 1970, "Translation and Underlying Structure II: Pronominalization and Reference," *NOT* 38:3-10

Fuller, Daniel P., 1967, "Delimiting and Interpreting the Larger Literary Units," *NOT* 28:2-12

Fuller, Daniel P., 1973, "Analysis of Romans 11:11-32," *NOT* 48:2-4

Gutt, Ernst-August, 1973, "Structural Phenomena in Acts 22: 6-11," *NOT* 48:11-23

Harbeck, Warren A., 1970, "Mark's Use of GAR in Narration," *NOT*, 38:10-15

Hollenbach, Bruce, 1969, "A Method for Displaying Semantic Structure," *NOT* 31:22-34

Longacre, Robert E., 1972, "Some Implications of Deep and Surface Structure Analysis for Translation," *NOT* 45:2-10

Nida, Eugene A., 1952, "A New Methodology in Biblical Exegesis," *TBT* 3/2, 97-111

Nida, 1964, 57-79

Nida and Taber, 1969, 39-55

Thomas, David, 1972, "Comments on Sentences, Propositions, and Notes on Translation 37," *NOT* 45:11-14

Toussaint, Stanley D., 1966, "A Proper Approach to Exegesis," *NOT* 20:1-6

Toussaint, Stanley D., 1967, "A Methodology of Overview," *NOT* 26:3-6

Tuggy, John, 1969, "Translation Procedure Used on Acts and James in Candoshi," *NOT* 34:3-31

SECTION 1. ANALYZING THE SURFACE STRUCTURE

A. *Analyzing "work of . . . ."* "Surface structure is what may be termed 'multifunctional.' That is to say, a given grammatical construction may signal different meanings, depending on the context; a lexical item also can have a number of senses. Further, and more significant, a given word or expression may be fulfilling several functions simultaneously" (Beekman-Callow, 1974, 270-71).

All of the following contain the genitive construction "work of . . . ." Study each passage and reword it so as to give the meaning of the construction.

Example: John 9:4
We must work *the works of him who sent me.*
We must do what the one who sent me wants us to do.

1) John 6:29
This is *the work of God,* that you believe in him whom he has sent.

2) John 9:3
It was not that this man sinned, or his parents, but that *the works of God* might be manifest in him.

3) John 10:37

   If I am not doing *the works of my Father,* then do not believe me.

4) Rom. 14:20

   Do not, for the sake of food, destroy *the work of God.*

5) Gal. 2:16

   yet who know that a man is not justified by *works of the law* but through faith in Jesus Christ

6) Phil. 2:30

   for he nearly died for the *work of Christ*

7) 2 Thess. 1:11

   that our God may make you worthy of his call, and may fulfill every good resolve and *work of faith* by his power

8) Gal. 5:19

   Now the *works of the flesh* are plain.

9) 1 John 3:8

   The reason the Son of God appeared was to destroy *the works of the devil.*

B. *Analyzing "love of . . . ."* In each of the following the genitive construction "love of . . ." occurs. Reword the passage so as to give the meaning of the genitive construction.

Example: Rom. 8:35

   Who shall separate us from the *love of Christ?*

   Who shall separate us from the love which Christ has for us?

1) Luke 11:42

   "But woe to you Pharisees! for you neglect justice and *the love of God.*

2) John 5:42

   But I know that you have not *the love of God* within you.

3) Rom. 5:5

   and hope does not disappoint us, because *God's love* has been poured into our hearts through the Holy Spirit

4) Rom. 15:30
I appeal to you, brethren, by our Lord Jesus Christ and by *the love of the Spirit.*

5) 2 Cor. 5:14
For the *love of Christ* controls us.

6) 2 Cor. 13:11
The God of love and peace will be with you.

7) Eph. 3:19
to know *the love of Christ* which surpasses knowledge

8) 1 John 2:5
but whoever keeps his word, in him truly *the love of God* is perfected (KJV)

9) 1 John 5:3
for this is *the love of God*

10) Jude 21
keep yourselves in *the love of God*

C. *Identifying the underlying meaning of identical grammatical structures.* In each of the following, two or three verses are cited in which the same grammatical construction is used but the underlying meaning is distinct. Reword each passage so as to show the difference in meaning.

Example: Luke 18:27
The things which are impossible *with men* are possible *with God* (KJV).
Things which men are not able to do, God is able to do.

2 Peter 3:8
With the Lord one day is as a thousand years.
The Lord perceives one day and a thousand years as if they were exactly the same.

1) Acts 21:21
They have been told that you teach all the Jews who are *among the Gentiles* to forsake Moses.
Rom. 2:24
The name of God is blasphemed *among the Gentiles* because of you.

Acts 15:12
They related what signs and wonders God had done through them *among the Gentiles.*

2) Philem. 13
I would have been glad to keep him *with me.*

Matt. 26:23
he who has dipped his hand in the dish *with me*

3) Luke 1:59
And *on* the eighth day they came to circumcise the child.

Luke 13:7
I have come seeking fruit *on* this fig tree.

4) Matt. 14:26
But when the disciples saw him walking *on the sea,* they were terrified.

Matt. 27:25
And all the people answered, "His blood be *on us* and *on our children.*"

Acts 4:5
On the morrow their rulers and elders and scribes were gathered together in Jerusalem.

D. *Identifying State and Event propositions.* "A proposition is the minimal semantic unit consisting of a concept or a combination of concepts which communicates an *Event* or a *Relation.*

"On the basis of this definition, two different classes of propositions can be distinguished: those which have an Event central are called Event propositions, and those which have a Relation central are called State propositions . . . . An *Event proposition* communicates an Event and consists of any other concepts that are related to that Event . . . . A *State proposition* communicates a Relation, either between two concepts belonging to the same semantic class, or between an Abstraction and a Thing or Event . . . ." (Beekman-Callow, 1974, 273-74, italics added).

The following propositions are taken from the propositional display of the book of Jude presented in *NOT* 37 by Richard Blight. Which of these are State propositions and which are Event propositions?

Example: Jude 1
  I am Jude.
    State proposition
  I serve Christ.
    Event proposition

1) God called you.

2) and they are ungodly

3) He is our only Master and Lord

4) that God destroyed some of the people of Israel

5) in order that God will judge them

6) Michael is the archangel

7) and because they rebelled against (authority)

8) these men are (dangerous to the believers)

9) because you let them feast together with you

10) (He was) in the seventh generation from Adam

E. *Identifying implicit Events.* In each of the following passages some Event(s) have been left implicit and some Event(s) are grammatically nouns (abstract nouns). List all the Events for each passage, including those which are only implicit. Then indicate who the agent of each Event is.

1) Matt. 2:7

2) John 4:12

3) Luke 2:4, 5

4) Col. 1:6-8

F. *Identifying Developmental and Supporting propositions.* "Propositions may be classified according to their function within discourse. They may serve either to develop or to support another semantic unit. There are thus Developmental propositions and Supporting propositions" (Beekman-Callow, 1974, 274).

The following is a section of the semantic display of propositions occurring in Colossians chapter 1. No indentation is included since this would show the relationships of a Supporting proposition. Classify each proposition as either Developmental or Supporting.

Developmental propositions are always related by Addition; Supporting propositions are always related by Association.

Colossians 1:1-3

    I, who am Paul
    who is an apostle
    who represents Jesus Christ
    because God chose me
    who is accompanied by Timothy
    who is our brother
    we greet you
    who are saints
    and who are our brothers in Christ
    who live in Colossae
    may God act in grace toward you
    He is our father
    may God impart peace to you

G. *Identifying paragraph boundaries.* None of the references listed below is the beginning of a new paragraph. Study the passage carefully and decide where the paragraph that includes the verse given begins and ends. Use a New Testament that does not have paragraph divisions.

1) Acts 13:10

2) 1 Cor. 11:11

3) 2 Cor. 5:9

4) 2 Cor. 7:12

5) Col. 3:6

6) Col. 4:1

H. *Identifying sections.* Identify the four major sections of 1 Corinthians, which are indicated by repetition of the same Theme proposition. What is that Theme proposition?

I. *Identifying the Theme propositions in Acts.* Toussaint (*NOT* 26, 5) outlines the book of Acts as follows:

    I. The witness in Jerusalem 1:1 – 6:7
    II. The witness in all Judea and Samaria 6:8 – 9:31
    III. The witness to the extremity of the earth 9:32 – 28:31

    A. The extension of the church at Antioch 9:32–12:24

    B. The extension of the church in Asia Minor 12:25– 16:5

    C. The extension of the church in the Aegean Area 16:6– 19:20

    D. The extension of the church to Rome 19:21 – 28:31

Study the verse ending each section and identify the Theme proposition which indicates the close of each of these large units of the discourse.

J. *Section or paragraph markers.* Find two examples in the New Testament where each of the following devices mark the beginning of a new section or a new paragraph:

    1) conjunction

    2) change of setting

    3) rhetorical question

    4) vocative

SECTION 2. PRACTICE IN WRITING PROPOSITIONS *(optional)*

A. *Writing propositions.* Rewrite the following passages in propositions.

    Example: Luke 24:13, 14

        That very day two of them were going to a village named Emmaus, about seven miles from Jerusalem, and talking with each other about all these things that had happened.

        That day two disciples were going to Emmaus. Emmaus was a village. Emmaus was seven miles from Jerusalem. The two disciples were talking to each other. The two disciples were talking about all the things that had happened.

    1) Matt. 10:1

        And he called to him his twelve disciples and gave them authority over unclean spirits, to cast them out, and to heal every disease and every infirmity.

    2) Matt. 17:2, 3

        And he was transfigured before them, and his face shone like the sun, and his garments became white as light. And behold, there appeared to them Moses and Elijah, talking with him.

3) Mark 1:35-37

And in the morning, a great while before day, he arose and went out to a lonely place, and there he prayed. And Simon and those who were with him followed him, and they found him and said to him . . . .

B. *Writing Romans 1:1-7 as propositions.* Romans 1:1-7 is one sentence in the rsv. First go through and write down every abstract noun which occurs in each verse. Next list all the genitive constructions by the verse in which they occur. If there are any passive clauses, list these and indicate in which verse they are found. These lists will help you to focus on some of the main things you will want to change in order to rewrite the passage into propositions. Rewrite in propositions making explicit the subject of every verb.

C. *Adjectival constructions, abstract nouns, and propositions.* Rewrite the following as propositions, eliminating the adjectival constructions and abstract nouns. Use only active verb constructions.

Example: 1 Peter 2:15

For it is God's will that by doing right you should put to silence the ignorance of foolish men.

God wills. You do right. You cause men to be silent. The men are ignorant. The men act foolish.

1) James 1:16

Do not be deceived, my beloved brethren.

2) James 1:11

For the sun rises with its scorching heat and withers the grass.

3) James 5:15

The prayer of faith will save the sick man, and the Lord will raise him up; and if he has committed sins, he will be forgiven.

4) 1 Peter 1:8

Without having seen him you love him; though you do not

now see him you believe in him and rejoice with unutterable and exalted joy.

5) 1 Peter 1:23

You have been born anew, not of perishable seed but of imperishable, through the living and abiding word of God.

D. *Metonymy, synecdoche, and propositions.* In the following passages identify the metonymy or synecdoche. Rewrite the passage in propositions, being sure to eliminate the figurative usage.

Example: Luke 1:32

The Lord God will give to him the throne of his father David.

"Throne" and "father" both are metonymy. God is Lord. God will cause Christ to rule. David ruled. Christ is a descendant of David.

1) Luke 1:49

He who is mighty has done great things for me, and holy is his name.

2) Luke 1:70, 71

He spoke by the mouth of his holy prophets from of old, that we should be saved from the hand of all who hate us.

3) Luke 3:6

All flesh shall see the salvation of God.

4) Acts 2:36

Let all the house of Israel therefore know assuredly that God has made him both Lord and Christ, this Jesus whom you crucified.

5) Col. 4:18

I, Paul, write this greeting with my own hand. Remember my fetters.

E. *Figures of speech and propositions.* In each of the following passages there is at least one figure of speech. Identify the figures of speech and then write them as propositions, eliminating the figurative usage. You may, however, use a simile in your proposition.

Example: Mark 5:34

And he said to her, "Daughter, your faith has made you well."

"Faith" is a personification.
Jesus spoke to the woman.
You believed. God healed you.

1) Luke 3:22

The Holy Spirit descended upon him in bodily form, as a dove, and a voice came from heaven, "Thou art my beloved Son; with thee I am well pleased."

2) Luke 4:20

And he closed the book, and gave it back to the attendant, and sat down; and the eyes of all in the synagogue were fixed on him.

3) Acts 15:21

For from early generations Moses has had in every city those who preach him, for he is read every sabbath in the synagogues.

4) Col. 2:14

God cancelled the bond which stood against us with its legal demands; this he set aside, nailing it to the cross.

F. *Metaphors, genitive constructions and propositions.* The following metaphors occur in a genitive construction. Change the construction to a proposition without changing the metaphor.

Example: Amos 6:12

fruit of righteousness

Righteousness produces fruit.

1) John 1:29

"Behold, the *Lamb of God*, who takes away the sin of the world!"

2) Eph. 2:20

built upon the *foundation of the apostles* and prophets

3) Eph. 6:11

Put on the whole *armor of God*.

4) Phil. 1:11
   filled with the *fruits of righteousness*

5) James 1:12
   He will receive the *crown of life*.

G. *Review*. Rewrite the following passage in propositions. Notice that there are a number of metaphors in the passage. Change the metaphors to similes or nonfigurative expressions.

James 1:12-15
   Blessed is the man who endures trial, for when he has stood the test he will receive the crown of life which God has promised to those who love him. Let no one say when he is tempted, "I am tempted by God"; for God cannot be tempted with evil and he himself tempts no one; but each person is tempted when he is lured and enticed by his own desire. Then desire when it has conceived gives birth to sin; and sin when it is full-grown brings forth death.

H. *Stating propositions*. Restate each of the following passages in the form of propositions:

1) 1 Thess. 1:1-4   6) Mark 8:22-26

2) Acts 7:12, 13   7) Mark 15:42-47

3) John 4:7   8) Titus 1:1-3

4) Rev. 2:9   9) 1 John 5:13-17

5) Acts 5:1-6   10) Rev. 22:1-5

CHAPTER 18

Relations Between Propositions

TEXT: Beekman-Callow, 1974, chapter 18

ADDITIONAL READING:

Ballard, D. Lee, 1973, "On the Translation of Greek Relationals," *NOT* 47:18-21

Ballard, D. Lee; Conrad, Robert J; and Longacre, Robert E., 1971, "The Deep and Surface Grammar of Interclausal Relations," *Foundations of Language* 7:70-118

Beekman, John, 1970, "Propositions and Their Relations Within a Discourse," *NOT* 37:6-16

Callow, Kathleen, 1970, "More on Propositions and Their Relations Within a Discourse," *NOT* 37:17-27

Deibler, Ellis W., 1966, "Comparative Constructions in Translation," *NOT* 22:4-10

Greenlee, J. Harold, 1962, " 'If' in the New Testament," *TBT* 13/1, 39-43

Jamieson, Carole, 1970, "The Relations of Modern Mathematical Logic," *NOT* 37:3-5

Hollenbach, Barbara E., 1973, "A Preliminary Semantic Classification of Temporal Concepts," *NOT* 47:3-8

Hollenbach, Barbara E., 1973, "Some Further Thoughts on Relations Between Propositions," *NOT* 47:9-11

Lithgow, David R., 1973, "New Testament Usage of the Function Words *Gar* and *Ei*," *NOT* 47:16-18

Roberts, J. W., 1964, "Some Aspects of Conditional Sentences in the Greek New Testament," *TBT* 15/2, 70-9

SECTION 1. ADDITION

A. *Chronological sequence versus simultaneity.* "The type of ADDITION that occurs between developmental propositions is controlled to a considerable extent by the type of discourse in which they occur. In narrative material, many of the propositions are related by one of the two time relations, sequence or simultaneity" (Beekman-Callow, 1974, 289).

"The label of Chronological sequence identifies the type of ADDITION in which two propositions follow each other in time in the referential world" (Ibid., 291).

"Two events are regarded as simultaneous if they overlap with one another in time in the referential world of the discourse. Events in sequence do *not* overlap at all; simultaneous Events always overlap to some extent, either partially or completely" (Ibid., 292).

Study each of the following passages and then restate in propositional form. Is the relation between the two propositions in the passage that of chronological sequence or simultaneity?

Example: Mark 1:31
  And he took her by the hand, and lifted her up.
  He took hold of her hand/he lifted her up. Chronological sequence

1) Mark 1:31
  The fever left her; and she served them.

2) Mark 1:35
  He rose and went out to a lonely place, and there he prayed.

3) Mark 3:5
  He stretched it out, and his hand was restored.

4) Mark 3:7
  Jesus withdrew with his disciples to the sea, and a great multitude from Galilee followed.

5) Mark 3:13
  And he went up into the hills, and called to him those whom he desired; and they came to him.

6) Mark 3:31
  His mother and his brothers came; and standing outside, they sent to him.

7) Mark 5:13

So he gave them leave. And the unclean spirits came out, and entered into the swine; and the herd . . . rushed down the steep bank into the sea, and were drowned in the sea.

B. *Other types of Addition.* ADDITION may consist of listing alternatives as in Romans 14:21, ". . . anything whereby thy brother stumbleth, or is offended, or is made weak." ADDITION is also the relation between the two halves of a conversation. This type of ADDITION is called conversational exchanges. In section A above, chronological sequence and simultaneity were exemplified. There is also a fifth type of ADDITION, that of relating two or more propositions which have the same relation to some other proposition (matched support).

Study the following passages to identify the type of ADDITION which occurs. The passage is first quoted from the RSV and then the propositions for the same material are given. Which of these five types occurs in each of the passages that follow?

a) chronological sequence

b) simultaneity

c) alternation

d) conversational exchanges

e) matched support

Example: Mark 4:28

first the blade, then the ear, then the full grain in the ear

first the blade appears/then the ear appears/then the grain appears in the ear

These three propositions are in a relationship of chronological sequence.

1) Mark 4:4

Some seed fell along the path, and the birds came and devoured it.

some seed fell on the path/birds came/the birds ate the seed

2) Luke 22:38

And they said, "Look, Lord, here are two swords." And he said to them, "It is enough."

They said to him . . ./He said to them . . .

3) 1 Thess. 5:10
   so that whether we wake or sleep we might live with him
   whether we are awake/or whether we are asleep

4) Mark 4:7
   Other seed fell among thorns and thorns grew up and
   choked it.
   other seed fell among thorns/the thorns grew up/they
   choked it

5) Col. 2:13
   dead in trespasses and the uncircumcision of your flesh
   spiritually dead/because you had sinned/and because
   you were not people who followed God

7) Phil. 1:27
   so that whether I come and see you or am absent
   whether I come to see you/or whether I remain absent

8) Mark 4:37-41
   In the following identify as many of the relationships listed
   above as you can. There will be some propositions related by
   certain relations that you have not yet studied. You may skip
   these.
   And a great storm of wind arose, and the waves beat into
   the boat, so that the boat was already filling. But he was
   in the stern, asleep on the cushion, and they woke him and
   said to him, "Master, do you not care if we perish?" And
   he awoke and rebuked the wind.

SECTION 2. SPECIFIC TYPES OF SUPPORT RELATIONS

A. *Support propositions that clarify and are distinct in meaning.*
There are support propositions that are distinct in meaning from
the propositions they support and that serve to clarify. In each
of the following there is a support proposition that functions to
clarify another proposition. Identify this support proposition and
state whether the relation is that of *manner, comparison,* or *contrast.* You may want to write out the propositions before stating
the relation.

   Example: Matt. 12:13
   and it was restored, whole like as the other
   "It is like the other" is a support proposition. The relation
   is that of comparison.

1) Col. 3:13
   forgiving each other; as the Lord has forgiven you

2) Jude 10
   they know by instinct as irrational animals do

3) Jude 20
   pray in the Holy Spirit
   (You must pray/let the Holy Spirit guide you)

4) Jude 23
   hating even the garment spotted by the flesh
   hate what evil he does/like one hates a filthy garment

B. *Support propositions that clarify and are similar in meaning.*
In A above we dealt with propositions that are distinct in meaning and that clarify. We turn now to support propositions that
are *similar* in meaning and that clarify. "This group of relations
is distinguished by the fact that there is an 'overlap' in content
between the two related propositions and this 'overlap' is an
essential part of the relation. The overlap may involve Things,
Events, or Abstractions, or any combination of them. However,
the overlap is not necessarily one of grammatical or lexical form;
the overlap may be different in form, but the same in meaning"
(Beekman-Callow, 1974, 297).

This group of relations includes *equivalence, generic-specific,
amplification-contraction.* This third group includes summaries,
leading questions, and rhetorical questions that occur with an
answer. The first group includes both synonymous expressions
and negated antonyms. For the purpose of this drill classify the
relation between the two propositions in each of the following
by the three main categories. If the passage contains more than
two propositions, select two propositions that may be subsumed
under one of these three main categories.

a) equivalence
b) generic-specific
c) amplification-contraction

Example: Luke 9:36
   and they kept silence and told no one
      equivalence

1) Matt. 16:6
   Take heed and beware of the leaven of the Pharisees and Sadducees.

2) Rom. 3:1-2
   Then what advantage has the Jew? Or what is the value of circumcision? Much in every way.

3) Acts 2:23
   This Jesus, delivered up according to the definite plan and foreknowledge of God, you crucified and killed by the hands of lawless men.

4) Rom. 3:27
   On what principle? On the principle of works? No, but on the principle of faith.

5) Acts 10:34
   And Peter opened his mouth and said . . . .

6) Acts 25:11
   If then I am a wrongdoer, and have committed anything for which I deserve to die . . . .

C. *Support propositions that argue.* The following drill has to do with support propositions that argue. "Each pair of propositions in this group is associated by the general relation of cause and effect. That is to say, one of the two propositions represents a cause, and the other the consequent effect. It is in this sense that one argues for the other by giving its causal antecedent or subsequent" (Beekman-Callow, 1974, 300).

Classify the relationships between propositions in the following passages on the basis of the chart on page 300 of the text. Have your book open to the chart as you study each passage. Then classify the relationhip as one of the following. (The order may be reversed between the propositions.)

   a) reason-result
   b) means-result
   c) means-purpose
   d) condition-consequence
   e) concession-contraexpectation
   f) grounds-conclusion

Example: James 4:2
  You do not have, because you do not ask.
    a) result-reason

1) Mark 3:25
   If a house is divided against itself, that house will not be
   able to stand.

2) Rom. 7:20
   Now if I do what I do not want, it is no longer I that do it,
   but sin which dwells within me.

3) Matt. 9:13
   I came to call sinners to repentance. (KJV)

4) 1 Thess. 5:9
   For God has not destined us for wrath, but to obtain salvation through our Lord Jesus Christ.

5) Rev. 5:9
   and by thy blood didst ransom men for God

6) John 9:39
   I came into this world, that those who do not see may see

7) 1 Thess. 3:5
   I sent that I might know your faith

8) Matt. 9:4
   But Jesus, knowing their thoughts, said . . . .

9) Col. 3:2, 3
   Set your minds on things that are above, not on things that
   are on earth. For you have died, and your life is hid with
   Christ in God.

10) Luke 17:3
    If your brother sins, rebuke him.

11) Col. 3:9
    Do not lie to one another, seeing that you have put off the
    old nature with its practices.

12) Mark 5:26
    (She) had spent all that she had, and was no better.

13) 1 Tim. 3:5
    If a man does not know how to manage his own household,
    how can he care for God's church?

D. *Condition of fact versus contrary-to-fact.* "The word 'if' cannot usually be translated by a single form into another language. A condition which is probably true or thought to be so by the speaker (condition of fact) is often translated differently than a condition which is probably not true (condition contrary-to-fact). The first will often be translated by a declarative clause rather than a conditional clause.

"For example, when Jesus says, 'And if I cast out demons by Beelzebub . . .' (Matt. 12:27), Jesus is hardly intending to imply that he does in fact cast out demons by Beelzebub. . . . On the other hand, Jesus' statement in John 14:3, 'And if I go and prepare a place for you . . .' is anything but uncertain and undependable . . ." (Greenlee, 1962, 39).

Study each of the following conditional sentences and decide if they are condition of fact or condition contrary-to-fact. Matthew 12:27 above is contrary-to-fact and John 14:3 is fact.

1) Matt. 22:45
   If David thus calls him Lord, how is he his son?

2) John 5:46
   If you believed Moses, you would believe me.

3) John 11:32
   Lord, if you had been here, my brother would not have died.

4) John 13:32
   If God is glorified in him, God will also glorify him in himself.

5) John 3:12
   If I have told you earthly things and you do not believe

6) John 15:19
   If you were of the world, the world would love its own.

7) Acts 3:9, 10
   If we are being examined today concerning a good deed done to a cripple, be it known to you all

8) 1 John 2:19
   For if they had been of us, they would have continued with us.

E. *Identifying types of conditional clauses.* "Both of the two previous types of clauses deal with definite events. . . . The third type of conditional clause which commonly occurs in the N.T. . . . deals with, either 1) a general condition which may occur at various times (e.g. 'if it falls into a pit on the sabbath,' Matt. 12:11) or 2) a future possibility (e.g. 'if I only touch his garment . . . ,' Matt. 9:21)" (Greenlee, 1962, 41).

This third class is called "conditions of contingency." Study the following to see which refer to definite events and are therefore either fact or contrary-to-fact and which do not refer to a definite event but are conditions of contingency.

Example: Matt. 4:9
All these I will give you, if you will fall down and worship me.

contingency

Matt. 4:3
If you are the Son of God, command these stones to become loaves of bread.

fact

1 Cor. 2:8
None of the rulers of this age understood this; for if they had, they would not have crucified the Lord of glory.

contrary-to-fact

1) Mark 3:25
And if a house is divided against itself, that house will not be able to stand.

2) Mark 13:22
False Christs and false prophets will arise to lead astray, if possible, the elect.

3) Luke 17:3
Take heed to yourselves; if your brother sins, rebuke him, and if he repents, forgive him.

4) 1 Cor. 14:37
If any one thinks that he is a prophet, or spiritual, he should acknowledge that what I am writing to you is a command of the Lord.

5) 1 Cor. 15:16
   For if the dead are not raised, then Christ has not been
   raised.

6) 2 Cor. 5:1
   For we know that if the earthly tent we live in is destroyed,
   we have a building from God.

F. *"Unless" clauses or conditionals.* A sentence of two clauses,
one of which contains *unless* and the other a negative (at least
implied), must often be translated as a conditional sentence.

Rewrite the following, using a conditional clause. Then state
whether the conditional clause is fact, contrary-to-fact, or contingency.

Example: Acts 27:31
   Unless these men stay in the ship, you *cannot* be saved.
   Cuicateco: If these men flee, you cannot be rescued.
   contingency

1) John 3:2
   No one can do these signs that you do, unless God is with
   him.

2) John 4:48
   Unless you see signs and wonders you will not believe.

3) John 6:53
   Unless you eat the flesh of the Son of Man and drink his
   blood, you have no life in you.

4) John 6:65
   No one can come to me unless it is granted him by the
   Father.

5) John 15:4
   As the branch cannot bear fruit by itself, unless it abides
   in the vine, neither can you, unless you abide in me.

6) John 19:11
   You would have no power over me unless it had been given
   you from above.

7) John 20:25
   Unless I see in his hands the print of the nails I will not
   believe.

8) Rom. 10:15

And how can men preach unless they are sent?

9) 1 Cor. 15:36

What you sow does not come to life unless it dies.

G. *Support propositions that orient.* "This group of propositions provides what can be termed background information, or the setting for another proposition. They give its orientation with respect to time, or place, or some other accompanying Event. Because the members of this group have this particular semantic function, they are often related to groups of propositions, such as paragraphs, by providing the orientation for the whole group, especially in narrative material" (Beekman-Callow, 1974, 309).

Classify the following support propositions that orient as to whether the orientation is that of (a) time (b) location, or (c) circumstance.

Example: Matt. 13:25

But while men were sleeping, his enemy came and sowed weeds.

"While men were sleeping" is a support proposition that orients as to *time*.

1) John 12:36

While you have light, believe in the light.

2) John 1:28

This took place in Bethany.

3) Acts 9:10

Now there was a disciple at Damascus named Ananias. The Lord said to him in a vision . . . .

4) Acts 8:25

Now when they had testified and spoken the word of the Lord, they returned to Jerusalem.

5) Luke 11:1

When he ceased (praying) one of his disciples said to him . . . .

6) Luke 9:37

On the next day, when they had come down from the mountain, a great crowd met him.

7) Luke 2:25
Now there was a man in Jerusalem, whose name was Simeon.

H. *Support propositions that are related to part of a proposition.* "In accounting for the relations of all the propositions in a paragraph, it is sometimes necessary to use three relations which link a whole proposition with only part of another proposition" (Beekman-Callow, 1974, 311).

These three relations are *identification, comment,* and *content.* Identify propositions that have these relations to some part of the proposition they support.

Example: John 6:50
This is the bread which comes down from heaven.
The proposition "comes down from heaven" is used to identify the bread and so the relation is one of *identification.*

1) Rev. 12:9
The great dragon was thrown down, the deceiver of the whole world.

2) Col. 1:4
because we have heard of your faith in Christ Jesus

3) Phil. 4:21
The brethren who are with me greet you.

4) Col. 2:12
You were also raised with him through faith in the working of God, who raised him from the dead.

5) John 17:24
Father, I desire that they also may be with me.

6) John 18:26
One of the servants of the high priest, a kinsman of the man whose ear Peter had cut off, asked . . . .

7) John 17:15
I do not pray that thou shouldst take them out of the world.

8) John 17:17
Consecrate them in the truth; thy word is truth.

I. *Propositional display of Colossians 1:1-5.* The following is a possible propositional display of Colossians 1:1-5. On the far right the first few relations have been labeled. Continue labeling the relations between propositions throughout the passage. Developmental propositions need not be labeled. (e.g., 1e, 2e, f). At the left a number has been given to each proposition. This includes the number of the verse in which it occurs and a letter to number the propositions within the verse.

1a	(I who am) Paul	IDENTIFICATION of I in 1e
b	(who am) an apostle	IDENTIFICATION of I in 1e
c	who (represents) Christ Jesus	COMMENT on apostle
d	because God willed it/chose me	REASON for b, c
e	I and brother Timothy (greet you)	
2a	who (are) in Colossae	IDENTIFICATION of you
b	who are saints	
c	and who are brothers in Christ	
d	who are faithful (to Christ)	
e	(May) God act in grace toward you	
f	and (may) God (impart) peace to you	
g	who is our Father	
3a	We always thank God	
b	who is the Father of our Lord Jesus Christ	
c	whenever we pray for you	
4a	because we have heard (from Epaphras)	
b	that you believe in Christ Jesus	
c	and that you love all the saints	
5a	because you look forward to (sharing with them)	
b	what is prepared (Gr: laid up) for you in heaven	
c	which (you came to know about)	
d	when you heard the true message	
e	which is the gospel.	

J. *Propositional display of Titus 1:5-16.* Study Titus 1:5-16 carefully. Then write out the propositions for this passage as was done for Colossians 1:1-5 above, and label the relationship.

SECTION 3. REVIEW

A. *Identifying potential translation problems.* Name at least one potential translation problem in each of the following passages. You may want to list more than one for some passages. Copy out the words that represent the problem you name.

Example: John 4:13
  Jesus said to her, "Every one who drinks of this water will thirst again."
  every one — may need to be plural rather than singular, e.g., all who (drink).

1) John 19:13
  When Pilate heard these words, he sat down on the judgment seat.

2) John 19:17
  So they took Jesus, and he went out, bearing his own cross.

3) John 19:19
  Pilate also wrote a title and put it on the cross; it read, "Jesus of Nazareth, the King of the Jews."

4) John 20:15
  She said to him, "Sir, if you have carried him away, tell me where you have laid him."

5) John 20:21
  Jesus said to them again, "Peace be with you. As the Father hath sent me, even so I send you."

6) John 20:26
  The doors were shut, but Jesus came and stood among them, and said . . . .

7) John 20:31
  These are written that you may believe that Jesus is the Christ.

8) John 21:7
  That disciple whom Jesus loved said to Peter, "It is the Lord!"

9) John 21:22
  Jesus said to him, "If it is my will that he remain until I come, what is that to you? Follow me!"

10) John 21:24
  This is the disciple who is bearing witness to these things, and who has written these things; and we know that his testimony is true.

B. *Identifying potential translation problems continued.* The following ten passages contain potential translation problems. Each passage contains a potential adjustment for one of the following: (a) ellipsis, (b) omission of clause, (c) genitive construction, (d) rhetorical question, (e) conditional clause — fact, (f) conditional clause — contrary-to-fact, (g) conditional clause — contingency, (h) obligatory possession, (j) extended use of number, (k) extended use of person.

Identify the potential adjustment from the above list. After telling what adjustment is involved, rewrite the passage, making the appropriate adjustment.

Example: John 15:4

As the branch cannot bear fruit by itself, neither can you.

Potential adjustment concerns *ellipsis.*

As the branch cannot bear fruit by itself neither can you bear fruit by yourself.

1) Mark 15:28

And the scripture was fulfilled, which saith, "He was numbered with the transgressors." (KJV)

2) John 8:28

So Jesus said, "When you have lifted up the Son of man, then you will know that I am he."

3) John 18:22

One of the officers standing by struck Jesus with his hand, saying, "Is that how you answer the high priest?"

4) John 18:23

Jesus answered him, "If I have spoken wrongly, bear witness to the wrong; but if I have spoken rightly, why do you strike me?"

5) 2 Cor. 1:3

Blessed be the God and Father of our Lord Jesus Christ, the Father of mercies and God of all comfort.

6) Matt. 19:17, 18

"If you would enter life, keep the commandments." He said to him, "Which?"

7) Rom. 7:20
Now if I do what I do not want, it is no longer I that do it, but sin which dwells within me.

8) John 10:30
"I and the Father are one."

9) 2 Thess. 1:4
Therefore we ourselves boast of you in the churches.

C. *Identifying adjustments that have been made in a translation.* Identify as many translation adjustments that have been made in the following translation as you can. This is a back-translation into English of the translation into Tepehua. Compare with the RSV or ASV.

John 1:35-44 (Tepehua):

³⁵The next day again John was standing with two of his men. ³⁶And he again saw Jesus where he was coming and said to them, "Look at that man who is going to be like God's lamb." ³⁷And those two men of John's when they heard what he said, well, immediately they followed Jesus. ³⁸And when Jesus turned around he saw those who were following him. He said to them, "What are you hunting for?" And they said to him, "Rabbi, where do you live?" Rabbi means teacher. ³⁹Well, he said to them, "Come. You will see where I live." And they went with him. They saw where he lived. Well, that day they stayed there with him since it was about four in the afternoon. ⁴⁰And those two who heard John's words and followed Jesus, well, one was called Andrew. He was the younger brother of Simon Peter. ⁴¹Well, Andrew immediately found his real brother who was called Simon. And he said to his brother, "We have found the Messiah." That means we have found the Christ, the one of whom it was said that God would send him here. ⁴²And immediately he took him to where Jesus was. When Jesus saw him he said to him, "You are Simon. You are the son of Jonas. You will be called Cephas." Cephas and Peter mean rock. ⁴³When the next day came, Jesus said that he was going to the land of Galilee. There he came across the one who was called Philip. And he said to him that he should follow him. ⁴⁴Philip lived in the town of Bethsaida. It was in the land of Andrew and Peter.

CHAPTER 19

Larger Semantic Units

TEXT: Beekman-Callow, 1974, chapter 19

ADDITIONAL READING:

Beekman, John, 1970, "A Structural Display of Propositions in Jude," *NOT* 37:27-31

Beekman, John, 1970, "Structural Notes on the Book of Jude (1)," *NOT* 37:36-38

Blight, Richard C., 1970, "An Alternative Display of Jude," *NOT* 37:32-36

Callow, John, 1970, "Structural Notes on the Book of Jude (2)," *NOT* 37:38-42

Fuller, Daniel P., 1967, "Delimiting and Interpreting the Larger Literary Units," *NOT* 28:1-12

Fuller, Daniel P., 1973, "Analysis of Romans 11:11-32," *NOT* 48:2-4

A. *Indentation format in a display.* In order to use displays of the semantic structure of a passage of Scripture, it is important to understand the symbolism of indentation as a way of showing rank.

The main proposition or propositions (developmental propositions) are placed furthest to the left and supporting propositions are indented to show this supporting relationship. Propositions are indented one more to the right than the propositions they support whether it is supporting a developmental proposition or another supporting proposition. Relations of identification and comment usually have double indentation for reasons discussed in the text.

Below, the propositions of a given passage are stated and the relations labeled but the display includes no indentation. Rewrite the display with the proper indentation to show the supportive relationships.

Example: Col. 1:13

13a Our Father has rescued us
  b so that we are no longer ruled by the evil one RESULT of a
  c and he has transferred us
  d so that we are now ruled by his Son   RESULT of c
  e whom he loves   COMMENT on Son

13a Our Father has rescued us
  b   so that we are no longer ruled by the evil one
  c and he has transferred us
  d   so that we are now ruled by his Son
  e   whom he loves

Col. 1:25

25a I (emphatic) minister to (the church)
  b because God appointed me to this office   REASON for a
  c in order that (I might help) you   PURPOSE of b
  d in order that I might make known to all people
     (Gk.: fill up) the message   PURPOSE of b
  e which (has been revealed) by God   IDENTIFICATION
                            of message

B. *Labeling relations in a display.* In each of the following the propositions are given and displayed with indentation to show supporting relationship. At the right, however, the kind of relationship is not specified but a blank appears where a relation marker is needed. Study the relationship and fill in the blanks. Be sure to include both the relation label and the propositions or word which it supports.

Example: Col. 1:28

28a I preach about Christ
  b I warn everyone with much wisdom
  c I teach everyone with much wisdom

d   in order that everyone will become
       spiritually mature (Gk.: in Christ)   PURPOSE of a, b, c

1)   Col. 2:18

18a Do not heed anyone
  b   who would (want to) condemn you   _____
  c   who advocates   _____
  d   that people should practice
         (so-called) humility   _____
  e   that people should worship angels   _____
  f   by talking about   _____
  g   things which he has seen (in visions)   _____
  h   because he is proud without reason   _____
  i   because he thinks only of   _____
  j   things which his lower
           nature wants   _____
       (Gk. of h, i, j: vainly puffed up by the
      mind of his flesh)

2)   Col. 3:5-9

5a   Stop (Gk.: put to death) yourselves
     (Gk.: your members on the earth)
     from doing (such evil deeds as)
  b   (Don't practice) (sexual) immorality
  c   (Don't be) indecent
  d   (Don't) lust   _____
  e   (Don't) desire (to do) evil
  f   And (don't) covet/be greedy
  g   inasmuch as (people) treat as gods
         (the things)   _____
  h   (which they covet)   _____
  i   just as (people) treat idols
         as gods (g-i Gk.: which is
         idolatry)   _____

6a   (Don't do those things)   _____
  b   because God will certainly punish
       (people)   _____

c	who habitually disobey (God) _____
d	because (they do) these things _____
7a	You also used to behave (like that) among them _____
b	when you lived _____
c	habitually (sinning) like that _____

8a But now you too get rid of/don't do
(Gk.: put off) all (evil) things

b (Don't be) angry

c (Don't have) passionate outbursts

d (Don't have) malice   _____

e (Don't) slander (people)

f (Don't use) abusive speech

9a (Don't) be lying to each other

b because you have gotten rid of (Gk.: put off) your evil nature (Gk.: old man) and the evil habits/evil things _____

c which it caused you to practice _____

3) Col. 3:12-14

12a Acquire (Gk.: put on) (these virtues)

b inasmuch as you are (people) _____

c whom God chose

d whom (God) has set apart/made holy _____

e whom (God) loves

f Be compassionate

g Be kind

h Be humble

i Be considerate   _____

j Be patient

13a Patiently bear with each other's (faults)

b Forgive each other

c whenever one of you has a complaint against another _____

d	just as the Lord forgave you	_____
e	you must forgive each other	_____
14a	Most important of all, love (each other)	_____
b	which will enable you to practice all these virtues (Gk.: as a bond) perfectly	_____

4) Titus 1:15, 16

15a	People respond to all things	
b	who are clean/pure	_____
c	which are clean/pure	_____
d	Other people do not respond to (things)	
e	who are defiled/unclean	_____
f	who do not believe (about Christ)	_____
g	which are clean/pure	_____
h	because their minds are defiled/unclean	_____
i	because their consciences are corrupted	_____
16a	(These people) say/profess	_____
b	that they know God	_____
c	but they deny	_____
d	that they know God	_____
e	by doing (evil) things	_____
f	because they are detestable	_____
g	and because they do not obey	_____
h	and because they are not fit/able	_____
i	that they do (things)	_____
j	which are good	_____

C. *Identifying larger semantic units in 3 John.* Study the book of 3 John. Identify the larger semantic units of this book and indicate your reasons for grouping as you do. Make a tentative propositional display of 3 John with indentation and propositional labels.

D. *Identifying larger semantic units in Luke 12.* Study Luke 12. Identify the larger semantic units of this chapter and indicate your reasons for grouping as you do.

CHAPTER 20

Analyzing and Displaying the Propositions Within a Paragraph

TEXT: Beekman-Callow, 1974, chapter 20

ADDITIONAL READING:

Beekman, John, 1970, "A Structural Display of Propositions in Jude," *NOT* 37:27-31

Fuller, Daniel P., 1967, "Delimiting and Interpreting the Larger Literary Units," *NOT* 28:1-12

Fuller, Daniel P., 1973, "Analysis of Romans 11:11-32," *NOT* 48:2-4

Hollenbach, Bruce, 1969, "A Method of Displaying Semantic Structure," *NOT* 31:22-34

Nida, 1964, 57-69

Nida and Taber, 1969, 33-55

A. *Identifying Event words.* In chapter 19 we were concerned with identifying the larger units within a discourse. "Having identified a paragraph, the next step is to go through it carefully identifying all the words or phrases which represent Events. This means not only the verbs (finite, participial, and infinite forms), but also the abstract nominals which represent Events" (Beekman-Callow, 1974, 327).

Identify the Event words in each of the following passages.

Example: Philemon 5
. . . because I hear of your love and of the faith which you have toward the Lord Jesus and all the saints.
Events are: hear, love, faith, have

1) Matt. 16:28
Truly, I say to you, there are some standing here who will

not taste death before they see the Son of man coming in his kingdom.

2) Matt. 18:14
   So it is not the will of my Father who is in heaven that one of these little ones should perish.

3) John 7:38
   He who believes in me, as the scripture has said, 'Out of his heart shall flow rivers of living water.'

4) Acts 3:14
   But you denied the Holy and Righteous One, and asked for a murderer to be granted to you.

5) Rom. 7:8
   But sin, finding opportunity in the commandment, wrought in me all kinds of covetousness. Apart from the law sin lies dead.

6) Col. 1:23
   provided that you continue in the faith, stable and steadfast, not shifting from the hope of the gospel which you heard, which has been preached to every creature under heaven, and of which I Paul became a minister

7) 2 Thess. 2:16, 17
   Now may our Lord Jesus Christ himself, and God our Father, who loved us and gave us eternal comfort and good hope through grace, comfort your hearts and establish them in every good work and word.

8) Heb. 3:16
   Who were they that heard and yet were rebellious? Was it not all those who left Egypt under the leadership of Moses?

9) Heb. 5:7, 8
   In the days of his flesh, Jesus offered up prayers and supplications, with loud cries and tears, to him who was able to save him from death, and he was heard for his godly fear. Although he was a Son, he learned obedience through what he suffered.

10) 1 Peter 5:1-2
    So I exhort the elders among you, as a fellow elder and a witness of the sufferings of Christ as well as a partaker in

the glory that is to be revealed. Tend the flock of God that is your charge, not by constraint but willingly, not for shameful gain but eagerly.

B. *Identifying implicit Events.* In the following passages identify the Event words and then look for other events that are implicit in the passage and therefore part of the semantic structure even though there is no lexical item in the surface structure.

Example: Phil. 1:3
    I thank my God
       Events: explicit—thank; implicit—worship
       I thank God whom I worship

1) John 6:11
Jesus took the loaves, and when he had given thanks, he distributed them to those who were seated; so also the fish, as much as they wanted.

2) Matt. 26:5
But they said, "Not during the feast, lest there be a tumult among the people."

3) John 2:10
He said to him, "Every man serves the good wine first; and when men have drunk freely, then the poor wine."

4) Matt. 2:7
Then Herod summoned the wise men secretly and ascertained from them what time the star appeared.

5) Acts 21:13
Then Paul answered, "What are you doing, weeping and breaking my heart? For I am ready not only to be imprisoned but even to die."

6) Matt. 26:25
Judas, who betrayed him, said, "Is it I, Master?"

7) 2 Tim. 1:7
For God did not give us a spirit of timidity but a spirit of power and love and self-control.

8) John 15:4
As the branch cannot bear fruit by itself neither can you.

9) Mark 4:28
The earth produces of itself, first the blade, then the ear, then the full grain in the ear.

10) Col. 1:2
To the saints and faithful brethren in Christ at Colossae:
Grace to you and peace from God our Father.

C. *Using verbs to express Events.* As discussed in chapter 14,
many events are expressed grammatically by means of abstract
nouns. All of these must be expressed as verbs in the semantic
structure. Restate each of the following passages, using an
active verb to express the Event ideas.

Example: Phil. 4:17
Not that I seek a gift
I do not say that because I seek that you give to me

1) 1 John 4:21
this commandment we have from him

2) Rev. 21:4
death shall be no more

3) Luke 12:58
go with your accuser

4) Philemon 21
confident of your obedience

5) Luke 2:47
all who heard him were amazed at his understanding and
his answers

6) Acts 4:12
there is salvation in no one else

7) Luke 4:18
to proclaim release to the captives

8) Matt. 24:31
they will gather his elect

9) Col. 1:8
he has made known to us your love

10) Luke 8:48
your faith has made you well

D. *Using verbs to express genitive constructions.* In order to
rewrite a passage with propositions, one must also be able to
express genitive constructions by using the Event as a verb and
making explicit the participants. Restate the genitive construc-

tions in the following phrases, using verbs and making participants explicit.

Example: Rom. 3:20
Through the law comes knowledge of sin.
Through the law we come to know that we have sinned.

1) Eph. 1:4
before the foundation of the world

2) Eph. 1:1
by the will of God

3) Rom. 15:33
the God of peace

4) Eph. 1:13
the word of truth

5) Rev. 11:6
the days of their prophesying

6) Mark 15:42
the day of preparation

7) Heb. 2:14
he who has the power of death

8) Luke 3:2
the word of God

9) James 1:22
be doers of the word

E. *Review.* As further review, restate the following passages,
expressing Event ideas as verbs. Where necessary, make implicit
ideas explicit.

1) 2 Tim. 3:4
lovers of pleasure rather than lovers of God

2) Phil. 1:3
in all my remembrances of you

3) Matt. 8:26
men of little faith

4) Matt. 11:12
men of violence

5) Heb. 2:15
through fear of death

6) Luke 1:10
   at the hour of incense

7) Luke 1:39
   a city of Judah

8) Col. 1:20
   the blood of his cross

9) Mark 14:3
   the jar of the ointment

10) Acts 1:19
    the inhabitants of Jerusalem

F. *Semantic display of propositions.* Now work through several passages, doing a complete semantic display of the propositions. Follow the steps given below.

Step 1. Identify and list the Event words in the paragraph.

Step 2. Construct the propositions based on these explicit Events.

Step 3. Construct any additional proposition based on implicit Events.

Step 4. Relate the propositions to one another in a semantic display.

Example: Mark 1:4
John preached a baptism of repentance for the forgiveness of sins.

Step 1: preach
         baptize
         repent
         forgive
         sin

Step 2: John   preached   (something)
         (John)   baptized   (the people)
         (the people) repented
         (God)   forgave   (the people)
         (the people) sinned

Step 3: none

Step 4: a John preached
         b   that the people should repent CONTENT of preach
         c   and that he will baptize them CONTENT of preach

| d | so that (God) will forgive them | RESULT of b and c |
| e | who had sinned. | COMMENT on them (the people) |

This semantic structure will, of course, be translated differently for every language.

Aguaruna says: John preached to the people, saying, "You have sinned. Repent and I will baptize you so that God will forgive you."

TEV says: John . . . preaching his message, 'Turn away from your sins and be baptized,' he told the people, 'and God will forgive your sins.'

Now apply the four steps to each of the following passages.

1) Jude 16

2) Eph. 2:8

3) 1 Peter 2:15

4) 1 Thess. 1:3

5) Eph. 1:7

G. *Translating into "Glish."* Translate two or more paragraphs of epistle material from the ASV into restructured English, which we shall call "Glish." Maintain the same thematic focus and participant emphasis so that the message remains intact. The following restrictions apply to Glish.

a) There are no abstract nouns.

b) There are no participles.

c) Extended usages of pronouns and kinship terms are misunderstood.

d) Metaphors are rarely used.

e) A literal rendition of English figures of speech will be misunderstood.

f) Idioms and idiomatic expressions of English must be recast.

g) Rhetorical questions are used only for self-deliberation or to scold another.

h) "of" and —'s mean ownership or a kinship relation.

i) Other grammatical and lexical devices of English may be used as necessary.

CHAPTER 21

The Organization of Discourse

TEXT: K. Callow, 1974, chapter 1

ADDITIONAL READING:

Barnwell, Katherine, 1974, "Vocative Phrases," *NOT* 53:9-17

Cromack, Robert E., 1968, "Language Systems and Discourse Structure in Cashinawa," Ph.D. dissertation, Hartford Seminary Foundation

Duff, Martha, 1973, "Contrastive Features of Written and Oral Texts in Amuesha," *NOT* 50:2-13

Grimes, Joseph E., 1972, *The Thread of Discourse,* Technical Report No. 1, National Science Foundation Grant GS-3180. Ithaca: Cornell University

Larson, Mildred L., 1965, "A Method for Checking Discourse Structure in Bible Translation," *NOT* 17:1-25

Lauriault, James, 1957, "Some Problems in Translating Paragraphs Idiomatically," *TBT* 8/4, 166-69

Longacre, Robert E., 1968, *Discourse, Paragraph and Sentence Structure in Selected Philippine Languages: Volumes I, II, and III,* U. S. Department of Health, Education and Welfare, Office of Education, Institute of International Studies, Santa Ana, Calif.: The Summer Institute of Linguistics

Longacre, Robert E., 1972, *Hierarchy and Universality of Discourse Constituents in New Guinea Languages: Discussion,* Washington, D.C.: Georgetown University Press

Nida, Eugene A., 1960, "The Bible Translator's Use of Receptor-Language Texts," *TBT* 11/2, 82-86

Sheffler, Margaret, 1967, "Results of Network Diagramming: as applied to the Revision of Mundurukú Mark," *NOT* 32:2-32

Taber, Charles R., 1966, "The Structure of Sango Narrative," *Hartford Studies in Linguistics*, No. 17, Parts I and II. Hartford, Conn.: The Hartford Seminary Foundation

SECTION 1. DISCOURSE TYPES AND FACTORS DIFFERENTIATING THEM

A. *Identifying discourse types.* "The Scriptures exhibit several different types of discourse. . . . If a message is to come across clearly, it must be appropriately worded. It is important that the translator encode each different type in the appropriate way" (K. Callow, 1974, 13). In order to do this encoding, the translator must know how to recognize different discourse types in the source. Review the following definitions of discourse types and then identify the type in each passage given. What factors affected your decision?

Narrative discourse recounts a series of events.

Hortatory discourse attempts to influence conduct.

Explanatory discourse gives detail about a person, situation, or activity, chronological factors having no major significance.

Argumentative discourse attempts to prove something to the hearer; it has no time-line, but tends to exhibit frequent contrast between two opposing themes.

Procedural discourse gives instructions concerning the accomplishing of a task or the handling of a situation. It is normally ordered in a time-line, but it is a projected time-line, referring to the future rather than the past.

Conversation differs from the other types in that more than one speaker is involved. In the New Testament this type occurs embedded in both narrative and argumentive discourse.

Example: 2 Tim. 4:1-5

    Hortatory — because of the many commands to live well.

1) Matt. 2:1-12

2) Rev. 7:9-12

3) Titus 3:12-14

4) Matt. 7:1-6

5) Rom. 4:1-12

6) Luke 9:12-14

7) Acts 7:2-34

8) Luke 18:18-30

9) Heb. 12:12-17

10) Acts 12:6-17

11) James 5:13-15

12) James 2:14-26

13) Luke 14:8-11

14) Matt. 22:41-46

15) 1 Cor. 14:34,35

B. *Changing first person to third.* A major factor differentiating discourse types is their person orientation. Narrative discourse is normally told in either first or third person according to whether the narrator did or did not participate in the events narrated. In general, this accords with New Testament usage and causes no problems, but fairly frequently in the New Testament a narrator will refer to himself in the third person. (See section on "Examples of Translating Secondary Senses," [Beekman-Callow, 1974, pp. 106-16].)

Assume that you are translating into a language where third person may not be used for first person. Rewrite the following passages, changing to first person and making all corresponding changes.

Example: John 1:15
> You will see heaven opened and the angels of God ascending and descending upon the Son of man.
>
> Aguaruna: You will see the door of heaven opened and those sent from God descending and ascending at the place where I am, the one who was born becoming man.

1) John 20:1-10

2) John 3:13-15

3) Matt. 25:31-46

C. *Changing third person to first.* There are, however, languages in which a narrator talks about himself in the third person. When this is the case, some passages that are told in the first person in the source language may need to be adjusted to third person in the translation. Rewrite Acts 22:6-16 so that Paul is talking about himself but using the third person.

D. *Hortatory discourse.* In Bontoc of the Philippines an exhortation is stated in second person singular when it is an exhortation to perform an activity, in first person dual when it is exhortation to better character. Which of the following are exhortations to perform an activity and which to better character? Rewrite using the form which Bontoc would use.

> Example: Col. 4:16
>> And when this letter has been read among you, have it read also in the church of the Laodiceans.
>
> Col. 2:6
>> As therefore you received Christ Jesus the Lord, so live in him.
>
>> Col. 4:16   exhortation to perform an activity
>> Col. 2:6   exhortation to better character (This would be translated then: As therefore we [dual] received Christ Jesus the Lord, so let us [two] live in him.)

1) 2 Tim. 4:13
   When you come, bring the cloak I left with Carpus at Troas, also the books, and above all the parchments.

2) 2 Tim. 3:14
   But as for you, continue in what you have learned and firmly believed.

3) 2 Tim. 4:9
   Do your best to come to me soon.

4) 2 Tim. 2:23
   Have nothing to do with stupid, senseless controversies.

5) Col. 3:2
   Set your minds on things that are above, not on things that are on earth.

6) Col. 4:2, 3
   Continue steadfastly in prayer, being watchful in it with thanksgiving; and you should pray for us also.

7) Col. 3:5
   Put to death therefore what is earthly in you: immorality,

impurity, passion, evil desire, and covetousness, which is idolatry.

8) 2 Tim. 4:19
   Greet Prisca and Aquila, and the household of Onesiphorus.

9) Philemon 22
   At the same time, prepare a guest room for me.

10) Eph. 6:10, 11
   Finally, be strong in the Lord and in the strength of his might. Put on the whole armor of God.

E. *Explanatory discourse* also shows divergences as to which person is used in a given language. Some use second person — "you do this"; others, a general third person — "people do this." Rewrite the following explanatory passages, using a general third person:

1) Matt. 6:5, 6

2) Luke 14:8-11

F. *Person orientation of metaphors.* In many languages special subtypes of discourse, such as parables or examples, occur characteristically with a particular person orientation. For example, in Bahnar of Vietnam illustrative metaphors occur in first person.

Example: Mark 4:21
   Is a lamp brought in to be put under a bushel . . . and not on a stand?
   Bahnar: Do I ever bring in a lamp . . . ? Don't I put it on the lamp stand?

Rewrite the following passages, changing the third person to the first person:

1) Matt. 9:16, 17

2) Matt. 13:24-30

SECTION 2. SENTENCE LENGTH

A. *Dividing long sentences.* In the Greek the first three verses of 1 John are one long sentence. In order to translate into clear Villa Alta Zapoteco, this passage was broken into seven sentences, which are as follows:

We proclaim to you about Jesus Christ the person who is the word, he who gives eternal life. He was already present when the world began. We heard his words, we saw him and we looked at him and we touched him. He revealed himself to us and we saw him and we say that he lives eternally. And we proclaim to you that he is with our Father God and how he revealed himself to us. The person whom we saw and heard his words, we proclaim to you what he is like, in order that our head-hearts may be one. Truly our head-hearts are one with the head-heart of our Father God and with the head-heart of his son Jesus Christ.

Assume that you are going to translate into Villa Alta Zapotec. Study the following passages to see how you might break the one long sentence down into shorter sentences and still preserve all the relationships and meaning of the original. Rewrite the passage, using three or more sentences for each passage. (Use RSV or ASV.)

1) John 15:16

2) Mark 1:6, 7

3) Luke 8:1-3

4) Titus 1:1-4

5) Acts 1:1-4 (Try to make six or more sentences.)

6) Acts 10:36-38

7) Acts 17:30, 31

8) Rom. 1:1-7

9) 1 Thess. 3:1-3

10) 1 Tim. 1:8-11

Other long sentences that could be used for practice are: Mark 4:11, 12, 16, 17; Luke 3:1-4; Acts 26:22, 23; Romans 1:29-32; 2:5-11, 14-16; 4:19-21; 15:30-32; 1 Corinthians 1:1-3; 3:12, 13; 2 Corinthians 6:3-10; Galatians 1:1-5; 1:13, 14; 2:3-5, 15, 16; Ephesians 1:3-14, 15-23; 2:1-3; 3:1-6, 14-19; 4:1-3, 11-16; 6:5-8; Philippians 1:3-7; 2:5-8; Colossians 1:9-18; 1:22-29; 2 Thessalonians 3:1, 2; Philemon 4-6; Hebrews 1:1-4; 2:2-4; 7:1-3; 12:1, 2; 1 Peter 1:3-5; 2:9, 10; and 3:18-20.

B. *Combining short sentences.* In New Guinea there are languages that have very long sentences. The clauses are run together by using participles, temporal clauses, etc. For this reason, when one is translating into these languages, he may have to combine two or three sentences into a single sentence. In each of the following, rewrite the passage as one long sentence rather than several shorter ones. Do not connect with *and*.

Example: Mark 6:1, 2

He went away from there and came to his own country; and his disciples followed him. And on the sabbath he began to teach in the synagogue; and many who heard him were astonished saying, "Where did this man get all this? What is the wisdom given to him? What mighty works are wrought by his hands!"

Going away from there, coming into his own country, his disciples following him, going into the synagogue to teach on the Sabbath, many hearing him, they being astonished said, "This man having been given wisdom, doing many mighty works, from where does he receive in order to do all this?"

1) Mark 5:14, 15

2) Mark 5:16-19

3) Mark 6:45-47

4) Mark 6:53-55

5) Mark 11:12-14

SECTION 3. INVOLVEMENT OF THE NARRATOR

Some languages make it obligatory that the relationship of the speaker to his material be specified at every point, as to whether he observed the events reported, knows them by hearsay, or has deduced them from evidence. In other languages this is not obligatory, but it is of relatively frequent occurrence.

Assuming that you are translating into a language which requires this specification of narrator involvement, study the following passages and try to decide if the speaker (1) observed the events reported, (2) knew them from hearsay, or (3) deduced them from evidence.

Example: John 2:1-11
John probably observed the events reported, since it says that
the disciples were there.

1) John 3:22

2) John 3:23-30

3) John 4:7-15

4) John 4:31-38

5) Acts 1:6-11

6) Acts 5:1-11

7) Acts 16:11-15

8) Acts 16:35-39

9) Acts 21:17-25

10) Acts 21:26

SECTION 4. VOCATIVES

A vocative phrase is a phrase of direct address to a person or
group of people, usually using a personal name or a title of some
kind. The vocative has various functions in the discourse and
often does not have the same function in the Receptor Language
as in the Source Language.

A. *Attitude of the speaker using vocative phrases.* One function
of the vocative phrase in the English and the Greek New Testa-
ments is to show the attitude of the speaker toward the person
to whom he is speaking. In each of the following, identify the
vocative phrase and indicate the attitude of the speaker that is
being conveyed.

Example: Acts 26:15
Who are you, Lord?
The term "Lord" shows an attitude of respect.

1) Luke 12:32
Fear not, little flock, for it is your Father's good pleasure to
give you the kingdom.

2) Acts 26:25

I am not mad, most excellent Festus, but I am speaking the sober truth.

3) Luke 12:20

But God said to him, "Fool! This night your soul is required of you . . . ."

4) Gal. 4:19

My little children, with whom I am again in travail until Christ be formed in you!

5) John 20:16

Jesus said to her, "Mary." She turned and said to him in Hebrew, "Rabboni!" (which means Teacher).

B. *Functions of the vocative phrase.* Study this list of functions of the vocative phrase. Then study the passages below to determine which vocative function is in focus in the passage. A single vocative phrase may have more than one function.

    a) To show the attitude of the speaker toward the person to whom he is speaking.

    b) To make a personal appeal by focusing attention on an individual or group of individuals. Proper names are often used.

    c) To focus on certain qualities of an individual or group.

    d) For rhetorical or stylistic effect.

    e) To mark off the sections of the argument — to recall attention or to signal the beginning of a new subject.

    f) To focus on certain classes of individuals in the audience.

Example: Luke 12:20

But God said to him, "Fool! This night your soul is required of you . . . ."

To show the attitude of the speaker.

1) 1 John 4:7

Beloved, let us love one another; for love is of God.

2) Acts 26:27

King Agrippa, do you believe the prophets?

3) Matt. 17:17
   O faithless and perverse generation, how long am I to be with you?

4) Luke 13:34
   O Jerusalem, Jerusalem, killing the prophets and stoning those who are sent to you!

5) John 20:16
   Jesus said to her, "Mary." She turned and said to him in Hebrew, "Rabboni!" (which means Teacher).

6) Luke 7:40
   Jesus answering said to him, "Simon, I have something to say to you."

7) Eph. 5:22
   Wives, be subject to your husbands.

8) Matt. 23:13
   But woe to you, scribes and Pharisees, hypocrites!

9) 1 Tim. 6:11
   But as for you, man of God, shun all this.

10) 2 Cor. 6:11
    Dear friends in Corinth! We have spoken frankly to you, we have opened wide our hearts. (TEV)

C. *Changing vocative phrases to a different grammatical construction.* It may be necessary to change the form of the vocative phrase in order to conform to the natural grammatical pattern of the receptor language. In many languages, vocative phrases that focus on particular qualities and thus carry information are translated by a separate clause or sentence.

Example: Matt. 6:30
   RSV: O ye of little faith!
   TEV: How little faith you have!

Rewrite the vocative in each of the following, using a nonvocative grammatical pattern.

1) Luke 19:17
   And he said to him, "Well done, good servant! Because you have been faithful . . . you shall have authority over ten cities."

2) Matt. 17:17

O faithless and perverse generation, how long am I to be with you?

3) Luke 13:15

Then the Lord answered him, "You hypocrites! Does not each of you on the sabbath untie his ox . . . and lead it away to water it?"

4) Matt. 6:30

Will he not much more clothe you, O men of little faith?

5) Matt. 8:29

What have you to do with us, O Son of God?

SECTION 5. QUOTATIONS WITHIN DISCOURSE

One aspect of narrative structure that varies greatly from language to language is the handling of quotations, that is, conversational style discourse within a narrative.

ADDITIONAL READING:

Ballard, D. Lee, 1974, "Telling It Like It Was Said," *NOT* 51, 28-31

Edgerton, Faye, 1965, "Relative Frequency of Direct and Indirect Discourse in Sierra Chontal and Navajo Mark," *NOT with Drills*, 228-31

Hawkins, Robert E., 1962, "Waiwai Translation," *TBT* 13/3, 164-66

Moore, Bruce R., 1973, "Some Comments on Questions," *NOT* 49:16-18

Peeke, Catherine, 1965, "The Gospel of Mark in Auca," *NOT with Drills*, 47-54

A. *Changing indirect speech to direct speech in Navajo.* In the Navajo language indirect discourse is invariably turned into direct discourse, even to the expression of thoughts and opinions (Edgerton, 1965, 228). Assume that you are translating into a language such as Navajo. How might you make direct quotations from the following indirect speech, substituting *say* or *said* for the word italicized?

Example: Mark 3:9
And he *told* his disciples to have a boat ready for him.
And he said to his disciples, "Get a boat ready for me."

1) Matt. 19:7
Why did Moses *command* one to give a certificate of divorce?

2) Mark 5:18
The man who had been possessed with demons *begged* him that he might be with him.

3) Mark 5:43
And he strictly *charged* them that no one should know this, and *told* them to give her something to eat.

4) Mark 7:26
She *begged* him to cast the demon out of her daughter.

5) Mark 10:48
And many *rebuked* him, *telling* him to be silent.

6) Luke 4:3
If thou art the Son of God, *command* this stone to become bread.

B. *Using "said" plus direct speech in Waiwai.* Hawkins makes the following statement about the Waiwai language of British Guiana: "We also began to realize that there was no proper word in Waiwai for various types of statements such as 'to promise,' 'to praise,' 'to deny,' etc. The promise or praise was merely quoted and so with the denial, and in each case this direct discourse was followed by the above-mentioned stem (*ka* meaning 'to say' or 'to do'). We heard such forms as these: *Kmokyasi men, mika harare*: 'I will certainly come, you said'; meaning 'You promised to come.' *Kanawa yenpotho okre, nikay*: 'It is a wonderful canoe, he said'; meaning 'He praised the canoe.' *Arihararo maki weesi, kekne*: 'I didn't take it, he said'; meaning 'He denied that he took it'" (Hawkins, 1962, 164).

Assume that you are translating into Waiwai and must use the word *said* with a direct quotation to translate *promise, praise (commend),* and *deny.* These words may not be used inside the quote but the context of the quote must carry the idea. How might you translate the following:

1) Matt. 14:7
   He promised . . . to give her whatever she might ask.

2) Luke 8:45
   And Jesus said, "Who was it that touched me?" When *all denied*, Peter said . . . .

3) Luke 12:9
   He who denies me before men *will be denied* before the angels of God.

4) Acts 3:9
   And all the people saw him walking and *praising* God.

5) Acts 4:16
   a notable sign has been performed . . . and *we cannot deny it*.

6) 1 Cor. 11:2
   I commend you, because you remember me in everything.

7) 1 Cor. 11:22
   What shall I say to you? *Shall I commend* you in this?

8) Titus 1:2
   eternal life which *God*, who never lies, *promised* ages ago.

C. *Using "said" plus direct speech in Chontal.* In Navajo and Chontal (of Mexico) command, beg, beseech, ask, tell, proclaim, publish, question, discuss, marvel, be amazed, deny, permit, desire, and other ideas are often expressed by a direct quote following a form of the verb *say*. For example, in Chontal:

Mark 1:5
   confessing their sins
   They said, "It's true, we've done evil" (Edgerton, 1965, 230).

Mark 8:32
   Peter . . . began to rebuke him.
   He said to Jesus, "Don't talk like that" (Edgerton, 1965, 231).

Assuming that you are translating into a language that uses a quotation with the verb *say* to translate the italicized words in the following, how might you state the direct quotation?

1) Matt. 8:34
   All the city came out to meet Jesus . . . they *begged* him to leave their neighborhood.

2) Matt. 27:58
   He went to Pilate and *asked* for the body of Jesus.

3) Mark 3:12
   And he *strictly ordered* them not to make him known.

4) Mark 5:10
   And he *begged* him *eagerly* not to send them out of the country.

5) Mark 6:6
   And he *marvelled* because of their unbelief.

6) Mark 9:18
   I *asked* your disciples to cast it out and they were not able.

7) Acts 9:27
   declared to them how on the road he had seen the Lord.

8) Mark 10:13
   And they were bringing children to him, that he might touch them; and the disciples *rebuked* them.

9) Mark 11:16
   He *would not allow* any one to carry anything through the temple.

10) Mark 15:11
    But the chief priests *stirred* up the crowd to have him release for them Barabbas instead.

D. *Using "said" plus direct speech in Auca.* "In Auca, of Ecuador . . . indirect quotations must almost always be rendered by direct quotations. . . . There are unsuspected complications in that the person and number of the direct quotations have to be decided from the context, this complexity being heightened by the fact that such renderings may produce quotes within quotes within quotes. This is an especially common problem because any expression of desire is also treated as direct discourse, the verb of desire being simply the verb 'to say' " (Peeke, 1965, 50).

Example: Mark 3:12
   But He charged them strictly not to make Him known.
   Jesus spoke like a chief, " 'You all keep quiet!' I say. Don't
   be telling who I am."

Assuming you are translating into Auca, rewrite the following
passages, using direct quotations. You will not necessarily need
quotes within quotes.

   1) Luke 7:36
   One of the Pharisees *asked* him to eat with him.

   2) Luke 22:31
   Satan *demanded* to have you, that he may sift you like
   wheat.

   3) Acts 3:14
   But you *denied* the Holy and Righteous One, and *asked* for
   a murderer to be granted to you.

   4) Acts 7:46
   David found favor in the sight of God and *asked* leave to
   find a habitation for the God of Jacob.

   5) Acts 9:1, 2
   But Saul *asked* him for letters to the synagogues at Damascus, so that if he found any belonging to the Way he might
   bring them bound to Jerusalem.

   6) Col. 1:9
   We have not ceased to pray for you, *asking* that you may be
   filled with the knowledge of his will.

   7) Rev. 9:6
   And in those days men will *long* to die, and death flies from
   them.

E. *Using direct speech for purpose clauses in Aguaruna.* In
Aguaruna, of Peru, not only are all indirect quotes and all expressions of thought handled by direct quotes, but all purpose clauses
are made into direct quotes. A direct quote plus "saying" indicates purpose.

Example: Titus 1:5
   This is why I left you in Crete, that you might amend what

was defective, and appoint elders in every town as I directed you.

> Aguaruna: I left you in Crete, "That which we did not completely cause to become good, you cause it to become good," saying: "You appoint leaders, that they be in each town," saying; that which I told you before, you do it like that.

How might you express the following purpose clauses in direct quotes in Aguaruna?

1) John 6:6
   This he said *to test him.*

2) Mark 3:2
   And they watched him, *to see whether he would heal on the sabbath.*

3) Mark 6:46
   He went into the hills to *pray.*

4) Mark 10:13
   And they were bringing children to him, *that he might touch them.*

5) Mark 12:2
   He sent a servant *to get from them some of the fruit.*

F. *Using direct speech for purpose clauses in Gahuku.* In Gahuku of New Guinea, purpose clauses are also turned into direct quotations, but the purpose clause must precede the main clause. Rewrite the following according to the Gahuku pattern.

Example: John 6:6
   This he said to test him . . . .
   Gahuku: "I will test him," saying, he said . . . .

1) Mark 15:32
   Let the Christ come down *that we may see* and believe.

2) Mark 16:1
   (They) bought spices, so *that they might go and anoint him.*

3) Rom. 1:11
   I long to see you, *that I may impart to you* some spiritual gift.

4) John 3:14, 15

The Son of man must be lifted up, *that whoever believes in him may have eternal life.*

5) Luke 1:3, 4

. . . to write an orderly account for you *that you may know the truth concerning the things of which you have been informed.*

G. *Changing direct speech to indirect in Nilotic languages.* There are also languages in which indirect discourse is preferred to direct discourse, and the changes must be made in that direction. Nida mentions this in discussing the Nilotic languages of Africa. *"Preference for indirect quotations.* The shift from direct to indirect discourse can be made easily, but the translator has to bear such matters constantly in mind. This does not mean, of course, that all direct discourse must be changed, but one should reflect something of the percentage of usage of the indigenous language" (Nida, 1955, 58).

Assume that you are translating into a language with a preference for indirect discourse. How might you change the following passages?

Example: Mark 10:2

And Pharisees came up and . . . asked, "Is it lawful for a man to divorce his wife?"

And Pharisees came up and asked him if it were lawful for a man to divorce his wife.

1) Mark 1:38

And he said unto them, "Let us go on to the next towns . . . ."

2) Mark 6:25

And she came in and asked, saying, "I want you to give me at once the head of John the Baptist on a platter."

3) John 1:22

They said to him then, "Who are you? Let us have an answer for those who sent us . . . ."

4) Luke 15:18

I will arise and go to my father, and I will say to him, "Father, I have sinned against heaven and before you."

5) Luke 4:12

And Jesus answered him, "It is said, 'You shall not tempt the Lord your God.'"

6) Matt. 21:25

And they argued with one another, "If we say, 'From heaven,' he will say to us, 'Why then did you not believe him?'"

7) Matt. 2:8

. . . and he sent them to Bethlehem, saying, "Go and search diligently for the child . . . ."

8) Heb. 10:9

Then he added, "Lo, I have come to do thy will."

9) Luke 17:23

And they will say to you, "Lo, there!" or "Lo, here!" Do not go, do not follow them.

10) 1 Cor. 15:35

But some one will ask, "How are the dead raised? With what kind of body do they come?"

CHAPTER 22

Grouping

TEXT: K. Callow, 1974, chapter 2

ADDITIONAL READING:

Fuller, Daniel P., 1973, "Analysis of Romans 11:11-32," *NOT* 48:2-4

Grimes, Joseph E., 1972, *The Thread of Discourse*, Technical Report No. 1, National Science Foundation Grant GS-3180, Ithaca: Cornell University

Ham, Pat, 1971, "Shifts from Linguistic Order," *NOT* 39:16-21

Lauriault, James, 1957, "Some Problems in Translating Paragraphs Idiomatically," *TBT* 8/4, 166-69

Longacre, Robert E., 1968, *Discourse, Paragraph and Sentence Structure in Selected Philippine Languages, Vol. 1.* U. S. Department of Health, Education and Welfare, Office of Education, Institute of International Studies, Santa Ana, Calif.: The Summer Institute of Linguistics

Longacre, Robert E., 1971a, "The Relevance of Sentence Structure Analysis to Bible Translation," *NOT* 40:16-23

Longacre, Robert E., 1971b, "Translation: A Cable of Many Strands," *NOT* 42:3-9

Longacre, Robert E., 1972, *Hierarchy and Universality of Discourse Constituents in New Guinea Languages: Discussion*, Washington, D.C.: Georgetown University Press, 93-160

Loriot, James and Hollenbach, Barbara, 1970, "Shipibo Paragraph Structure," *Foundations of Language* 6, 43-66

Nida, E. A., 1950, "The Most Common Errors in Translation," *TBT* 1/2, 52-54

Nida, 1947, 263-65, 271-74

Nida, 1964, 209, 10, 235

Trail, Ronald L., 1973, *Patterns in Clause, Sentence, and Discourse in Selected Languages of India and Nepal, Part 1, Sentence and Discourse*, Department of Health, Education and Welfare, Norman, Oklahoma: Summer Institute of Linguistics of the University of Oklahoma

Wallis, Ethel E., 1971, "Contrastive Plot Structures of the Four Gospels," *NOT* 40:3-16

Wallis, Ethel E., 1973, "The Rhetorical Organization of Luke's Discourse," *NOT* 48:6-12

Wilson, W. A. A., 1964, "Some Frequently Neglected Syntactical Features of West African Languages," *TBT* 15/1, 11-16

SECTION 1. GROUPINGS

A. *Changing order of clauses.* The necessity for adjustments in the order of words seems so obvious as scarcely to require mention. However, there are certain situations in which the shifts of order may not seem so vital, but in which they are nevertheless important if the translation is to be natural" (Nida, 1964, 235).

In Aguaruna, of Peru, the word order within the clause may vary considerably. However, the most frequent order, especially in narrative material is: time, subject, object, indirect object, location, manner, and (finally) predicate. The predicate may be a compound verb. Rewrite the following putting the clause units into this order.

> Example: John 4:7
> There came a woman of Samaria to draw water. Jesus said to her, "Give me a drink."
> In Aguaruna: A woman of Samaria, water drawing came, Jesus "Water me give, that I drink," said.

1) Mark 5:1
They came to the other side of the sea.

2) Mark 5:21
Jesus crossed again in the boat to the other side.

3) Mark 6:13
And they cast out many demons, and anointed with oil many that were sick and healed them.

4) Mark 8:27
   And Jesus went on to the villages of Caesarea Philippi; and
   on the way he asked, "Who do men say that I am?"

5) Mark 9:2
   After six days Jesus took with him Peter and James and
   John, and led them up a high mountain.

B. *Placing verbal complements before the verb.* In many languages the modifiers of the verb must always precede the verb.
Rewrite the following, putting all verbal complements just before
the verb.

Example: Luke 1:64
    And immediately his mouth was opened.
      His mouth was immediately opened.

1) Matt. 5:11
   utter all kinds of evil against you falsely

2) Matt. 5:25
   Make friends quickly with your accuser.

3) Matt. 13:26
   then the weeds appeared also

4) Acts 10:2, 3
   who gave alms liberally . . . and prayed constantly to God.
   About the ninth hour of the day he saw clearly in a
   vision

5) Rev. 2:16
   I will come to you soon.

C. *Placement of the vocative phrase.* In some languages the
vocative must always come at the beginning of the sentence, but
never within the sentence, since it would break the continuity of
the main idea. Rewrite the following, making this adjustment.

Example: Acts 10:13
    And there came a voice to him, "Rise, Peter; kill and eat."
      And there came a voice to him, "Peter, arise, kill and eat."

1) Luke 4:34
   "Ah! What have you to do with us, Jesus of Nazareth?
   Have you come to destroy us? I know who you are, the
   Holy One of God."

2) Luke 1:1-4
Read this passage and see what adjustment would have to
be made.

D. *Topic sentences.* "Paragraphs often start with a topic sentence,
which acts as a setting for the paragraph as a whole, or links the
paragraph to the rest of the discourse, or both. Often the topic
sentence indicates a change in temporal or locational settings, a
change of the participant in focus, or a preview of the argument
or activity of the paragraph (K. Callow, 1974, 22).

For practice in identifying paragraph divisions in the source
language, study each of the following sections of Scripture, listing
any sentence that is clearly a topic sentence. How does each
topic sentence function?

Example: Matt. 1:18
Now the birth of Jesus Christ took place in this way.
This topic sentence functions by giving a preview of the
narrative.

1) Matt. 1:18 – 3:17

2) Matt. 9

3) Matt. 13:53 – 15:39

E. *Paragraph divisions.* "Frequently, paragraphs end with a
terminal sentence. This may state the successful attaining of his
object by the main participant, or may summarize the situation
reached, or may simply consist of the final event of a series. Sometimes it consists of an explanation or comment, or some such
material which, as it were, steps aside from the main flow of the
paragraph. The terminal sentence is very differently marked in
different languages" (K. Callow, 1974, 24).

For practice in identifying paragraph divisions in the source
language, go through the sections of Scripture listed in point A
above, looking this time for terminal sentences. How does each
terminal sentence function other than as a terminal sentence?

Compare your answers for section A and section B. Does both
a topic sentence and a terminal sentence occur at each paragraph
break in the source material?

F. *Interpolations.* In each of the following passages, identify the
interpolation that occurs in the source material. All such material

will need to be carefully marked according to the receptor language rules, if confusion on the part of the readers is to be avoided.

Example: Mark 15:33-39
> The comment about the curtain being torn in two from top to bottom interrupts the main story. In Nung of Vietnam it was necessary to change the order of verses 38 and 39 because Nung paragraph structure observes strict unity of location and verse 38 involves a change of location. It is then necessary to show the time setting of v. 38 by saying, "When Jesus died, the veil was torn . . . ."

These parenthetical comments, which break into the sequence of event or argument, if kept in the same position or order in relation to the other clauses or sentences in the translation, may distort the meaning of the passage. Many of these are set off by parentheses but not always. Study each of the following and give a reordering and/or rewording that will eliminate any possible confusion on the part of the reader.

Example: Gal. 2:2
> I went up by revelation; and I laid before them (but privately before those who were of repute) the gospel which I preached among the Gentiles, lest somehow I should be running or had run in vain.
>
> I went up by revelation and I spoke privately before those who were of repute. Then I laid before the whole assembly the gospel which I preached . . . .

1) Acts 1:15, 16
> In those days Peter stood up among the brethren (the company of persons was in all about a hundred and twenty), and said, "Brethren, the scripture had to be fulfilled . . . ."

2) John 1:38
> Jesus turned, and saw them following, and said to them, "What do you seek?" And they said to him, "Rabbi (which means Teacher), where are you staying?"

3) John 7:22
> Moses gave you circumcision (not that it is from Moses, but from the fathers), and you circumcise a man upon the sabbath.

4) John 9:7
   . . . saying to him, "Go, wash in the pool of Siloam" (which means Sent). So he went and washed and came back seeing.

5) Acts 4:36, 37
   Thus Joseph who was surnamed by the apostles Barnabas (which means Son of encouragement), a Levite, a native of Cyprus, sold a field . . . .

G. *Chronological order.* Rewrite Acts 1:1-3, putting the events in chronological order.

H. *Order of clauses within sentences.* In some languages of New Guinea, the independent clause must come last in the sentence. All purpose, reason, conditional, and other dependent clauses precede the main clause. Rewrite the following according to this rule.

Example: Mark 1:22
   And they were astonished at his teaching, for he taught them as one who had authority, and not as the scribes.
   Because he taught them as one who had authority and not as the scribes, they were astonished at his teaching.

1) Matt. 9:36
   When he saw the crowds, he had compassion for them, because they were harassed and helpless, like sheep without a shepherd.

2) Matt. 10:26
   So have no fear of them; for nothing is covered that will not be revealed, or hidden that will not be known.

3) Mark 1:38
   Let us go on to the next towns, that I may preach there also; for that is why I came out.

4) Mark 3:2
   And they watched him to see whether he would heal him on the sabbath, so that they might accuse him.

5) Mark 3:9, 10
   And he told his disciples to have a boat ready for him because of the crowd, lest they should crush him; for he had healed many, so that all who had diseases pressed upon him to touch him.

I. *Thematic groupings.* "Instead of considering a discourse as a purely grammatical entity, consisting of ordered patterns of sentences and paragraphs, it is possible also to consider it as a drama, plot, or theme. In this case, the units are not determined by grammatical criteria, but by their significance within the story or argument as a whole. Thus in many instances the introduction can be clearly distinguished from the main argument, while within the argument itself there is a distinction between complication/conflict (the period of problem or conflict), climax, resolution, and evaluation. Digressions within a major theme, or interwoven minor themes may also be discerned. These various elements in discourse may also be found in various discourses in Scripture" (K. Callow, 1974, 26).

Study each of the passages below from the following points of view.

a) List events on the time-line and look for any events not mentioned in chronological order.

b) Note how participant reference is maintained. Are there instances where rules for English would suggest other forms?

c) Does this narrative have dramatic structure of introduction, complication, climax, resolution, and evaluation?

1) John 2:1-10

2) Matt. 15:29-39

3) Matt. 26:20-35

SECTION 2. CHRONOLOGICAL SEQUENCE

A. *Reordering chronologically.* In languages such as Greek and English the linguistic order does not need to match the historical order of events (the chronological or experiential order). But in some languages the linguistic order is the same as the experiential. In translating passages in which the linguistic order in the source language does not match the experiential order, the order may need to be changed. For example, Acts 2:23 had to be changed in Chuj of Guatemala from "You killed him, putting him on a cross" to "You put him on a cross. He died because of you."

For each of the following suggest a rewording that will follow the experiential order of events.

1) Mark 7:17
   And when he had entered the house, and left the people, his disciples asked him about the parable.

2) John 4:1-3
   Now when the Lord knew that the Pharisees had heard . . . he left Judea and departed again to Galilee.

3) John 4:39
   Many Samaritans from the city believed in him because of the woman's testimony.

4) Acts 5:30, 31
   The God of our fathers raised Jesus whom you killed by hanging him on a tree. God exalted him at his right hand.

5) Rev. 20:4, 5
   They came to life again and reigned with Christ a thousand years. The rest of the dead did not come to life again until the thousand years were ended. This is the first resurrection.

6) Luke 1:20
   And behold, you will be silent and unable to speak until the day that these things come to pass, because you did not believe my words, which will be fulfilled in their time.

7) Rom. 4:18
   In hope he believed against hope, that he should become the father of many nations; as had been told, "So shall your descendants be."

8) John 1:33
   I myself did not know him; but he who sent me to baptize with water said to me, "He on whom you see the Spirit descend and remain, this is he who baptizes with the Holy Spirit."

B. *Reordering for logical and chronological order.* Sometimes the order within a passage has to be changed to follow the logical order of the argument. In John 1:14, "And the Word became flesh and dwelt among us, full of grace and truth; we have beheld his glory, glory as of the only Son of the Father," the parenthetical phrase, "full of grace and truth" had to be put at the end of the verse in Aguaruna.

For each of the following suggest a rewording that will more closely follow the logical and/or chronological order of the argument.

Example: 1 John 2:16
All that is in the world is not of the Father, but is of the world.
Amuzgo: All that is in the world is of the world, but it is not of the Father.

1) John 1:10
He was in the world, the world was made through him, yet the world knew him not.

2) 1 John 4:1
Beloved, do not believe every spirit, but test the spirits to see whether they are of God; for many false prophets have gone out into the world.

3) 1 Thess. 2:13
And we also thank God constantly for this, that when you received the word of God which you heard from us, you accepted it not as the word of men, but as what it really is, the word of God, which is at work in you believers.

4) Mark 7:25, 26
But immediately a woman, whose little daughter was possessed by an unclean spirit, heard of him, and came and fell down at his feet. Now the woman was a Greek, a Syrophoenician by birth. And she begged him to cast the demon out of her daughter.

5) John 1:19, 20
And this is the testimony of John, when the Jews sent priests and Levites from Jerusalem to ask him, "Who are you?" He confessed, he did not deny, but confessed, "I am not the Christ."

CHAPTER 23

Cohesion

TEXT: K. Callow, 1974, chapter 3

ADDITIONAL READING:

Beekman, John, 1965, "Ambiguity or Obscurity of Pronominal Reference," *NOT* 16, 7-12

Grimes, Joseph E., 1972, *The Thread of Discourse*, Technical Report No. 1, National Science Foundation Grant GS-3180, Ithaca: Cornell University

Gibson, Lorna, "The Use of Role in Translation," *NOT* 16:34

Lauriault, James, 1957, "Some Problems in Translating Paragraphs Idiomatically," *TBT* 8/4

Kingston, Peter K. E., 1973, "Repetition as a Feature of Discourse Structure in Mamainde," *NOT* 50, 13-22

Larson, Mildred L., 1965, "A Method for Checking Discourse Structure in Bible Translation," *NOT* 17, 1-25

Sheffler, Margaret, 1969, "Results of Network Diagramming: as applied to the Revision of Mundurukú Mark," *NOT* 32: 2-32

Wheatley, James, 1973, "Pronouns and Nominal Elements in Bacairi Discourse," *Linguistics* 104:105-115

Wise, Mary Ruth, 1968, "Identification of Participants in Discourse: A Study of Aspects of Form and Meaning in Nomastinguenga," Ph.D. dissertation, The University of Michigan

A. *Lexical cohesion.* Selection of vocabulary items from a common semantic area contributes greatly to discourse cohesion. Obviously, if many of the words in a paragraph come from the same semantic domain, they contribute to the unity of that paragraph. Study the following paragraphs and make a list of the words used that have a relationship to one another and so add lexical cohesion to the passage.

Example: Mark 1:16-20
    sea, Galilee, fisherman, nets, boat; brother, son, father.

1) John 10:7-16

2) Rom. 2:1-3

3) John 4:1-15

4) John 21:4-8

5) 1 Cor. 13

B. *Tracing participants through the discourse.* "Once a participant has been suitably introduced, it still remains to refer to him correctly thereafter, and to make sure that it is always clear who performed each event" (K. Callow, 1974, 33).

Passages from Mark, chapter 2, in the RSV and TEV translations are printed below side by side. Compare the two versions carefully. For every noun or pronoun in the RSV list the corresponding translation in TEV. In each instance where the TEV uses a noun rather than a pronoun, state why you think this change was made.

Mark 2 RSV

¹And when he returned to Capernaum after some days, it was reported that he was at home.

²And many were gathered together, so that there was no longer room for them, not even about the door; and he was preaching the word to them.

³And they came, bringing to him a paralytic carried by four men.

Mark 2 TEV

¹A few days later Jesus came back to Capernaum, and the news spread that he was at home.

²So many people came together that there wasn't any room left, not even out in front of the door. Jesus was preaching the message to them

³when some people came, bringing him a paralyzed man, four of them were carrying him.

⁴And when they could not get near him because of the crowd, they removed the roof above him; and when they had made an opening, they let down the pallet on which the paralytic lay.

. . .

¹³He went out again beside the sea; and all the crowd gathered about him, and he taught them.

¹⁴And as he passed on, he saw Levi the son of Alphaeus sitting at the tax office, and he said to him, "Follow me." And he rose and followed him.

¹⁵And as he sat at the table in his house, many tax collectors and sinners were sitting with Jesus and his disciples; for there were many who followed him.

. . .

¹⁸Now John's disciples and the Pharisees were fasting; and people came and said to him, "Why do John's disciples and the disciples of the Pharisees fast, but your disciples do not fast?"

. . .

²³One Sabbath he was going through the grainfields, and as they made their way his disciples began to pluck ears of grain.

⁴Because of the crowd, however, they could not get him to Jesus. So they made a hole in the roof right above the place where Jesus was. When they had made an opening, they let the man down, lying on his mat.

. . .

¹³Jesus went back again to the shore of Lake Galilee. A crowd came to him and he started teaching them.

¹⁴As he walked along, he saw a tax collector, Levi, the son of Alphaeus, sitting in his office. Jesus said to him, "Follow me." Levi got up and followed him.

¹⁵Later on Jesus was having a meal in Levi's house. There were many tax collectors and outcasts who were following Jesus, and some of them joined him and his disciples at the table.

. . .

¹⁸On one occasion the followers of John the Baptist and the Pharisees were fasting. Some people came to Jesus and asked him, "Why is it that the disciples of John the Baptist and the disciples of the Pharisees fast, but yours do not?"

. . .

²³Jesus was walking through some wheat fields on a Sabbath day. As his disciples walked along with him, they began to pick the heads of wheat.

²⁴And the Pharisees said to him, "Look, why are they doing what is not lawful on the Sabbath?"

²⁴So the Pharisees said to Jesus, "Look, it is against our Law for your disciples to do this on the Sabbath!"

²⁵And he said to them, "Have you never read what David did, when he was in need and was hungry, he and those who were with him."

²⁵Jesus answered: "Have you never read what David did that time when he needed something to eat? He and his men were hungry . . . ."

C. *Identifying the antecedent.* Confusion often arises in analysis of the source language because it is not clear to whom or to what a particular pronoun refers. Study each of the following to determine who or what is the antecedent of the italicized pronoun. Rewrite, making the antecedent clear.

Example: 2 Kings 19:35
The angel of the Lord . . . smote . . . a hundred fourscore and five thousand; and when *they* arose early in the morning, behold, *they* were all dead corpses (KJV).
first *they* — Israelites; second *they* — Assyrians

1) Mark 2:15
And as *he* sat at the table in *his* house . . . . (Study the context of this passage and compare also Luke 5:29.)

2) Matt. 2:21
And he rose and took the child and *his* mother, and went to the land of Israel. (Informants in several languages have understood that Joseph took his own mother along.)

3) Luke 4:36
And *they* were all amazed.

4) Luke 4:39
and immediately she rose and served *them*

5) 1 John 2:13
I am writing to you fathers, because you know *him* who is from the beginning.

6) 1 Cor. 3:19
He catches the wise in their craftiness.

7) Acts 10:46
   For *they* heard *them* speaking in tongues and extolling God.

8) Acts 10:43
   To *him* all the prophets bear witness.

9) Acts 20:36-37
   And when he had spoken thus, he knelt down and prayed
   with *them* all. And *they* all wept.

10) Acts 21:6
    Then we went on board the ship and *they* returned home.

D. *Pronominal reference.* The pronominal referent in each of the
following passages is ambiguous. Study the context until you
know to whom or to what the pronoun refers.

Example: Matt. 15:2
   they do not wash their hands
      The closest antecedent of *they* is *elders.* However, the
      proper antecedent is disciples.

1) Matt. 28:18
   And Jesus came and said to *them.*

2) Acts 25:7
   the Jews . . . stood about *him*

3) John 1:15
   John bare witness of *him.*

4) Mark 9:20
   And *they* brought the boy to him.

5) Luke 2:12
   And *this* will be a sign for you.

6) Eph. 5:12
   For it is a shame to speak of the things that *they* do in
   secret.

7) Acts 19:28
   When *they* heard this they were enraged.

8) John 8:40
   This is not what Abraham did.

9) Acts 3:2

whom *they* laid daily at the gate

E. *Use of role.* "A common way of referring to a known participant is by his role, whether this be his family relationship ('the
father,' 'the firstborn'), his nationality ('the Hebrew'), his social
position ('the visitor'), his official position ('the ruler'), or whatever is appropriate in the context. Pame of Mexico, for instance,
makes frequent use of such terms, hence it is used very naturally
in translation. Acts 16:38, for example, reads in the KJV (following the Greek), 'And the sergeants told these words to the magistrates: and they feared, when they heard that they were Romans.'
The three uses of 'they' seemed ambiguous, though in Greek it
is clear that the first two uses have the same referent. In Pame
the ambiguity was resolved by the use of role terms, thus: 'the
magistrates were·afraid when they heard that the two prisoners
were Romans'" (K. Callow, 1974, 34).

In each of the following, substitute role for the noun or pronoun used in the source.

Example: Acts 21:40

And when he had given him leave, *Paul*, standing on the
steps motioned with his hand

the prisoner

1) Luke 1:15

for *he* will be great before the Lord

2) Luke 1:63

And he asked for a writing tablet, and wrote, "*His* name is
John."

3) Acts 7:21

and when he was exposed, Pharoah's daughter adopted *him*

4) Acts 7:9, 10

And the patriarchs, jealous of Joseph, sold him into Egypt;
but God was with *him*, and rescued him out of all his
afflictions.

5) Acts 8:30

So Philip ran to *him*, and heard him reading Isaiah.

6) Acts 9:33, 34

There he found a man named Aeneas, who had been bedridden for eight years and was paralyzed. And Peter said
to him . . . .

7) Acts 16:1, 2

A disciple was there, named Timothy, the son of a Jewish
woman who was a believer; but his father was a Greek. *He*
was well spoken of by the brethren at Lystra and Iconium.

8) Acts 12:4

And when *he* had seized him, he put him in prison.

F. *Fourth person.* In Trique, and other languages, there are
fourth person pronouns. If you are already talking about someone with a third person pronoun and another actor comes into
focus he is referred to, after he has been named, by fourth person
pronouns rather than third person.

Example: Mark 5:2, 6

"And when he had come out of the boat, there met him out
of the tombs a man with an unclean spirit who when *he* saw
Jesus . . . *he* ran and worshipped him."

Instructions: Assume you are translating into a language in
which fourth person, *nam*, is used rather than third for a newly
introduced third person if (1) the newly introduced person is
of the same gender and (2) of the same number. That is, fourth
is not used if the two participants are one masculine and the
other feminine or if the one is singular and the other plural.
Gender and number keep the persons straight without going to
the use of a fourth person; however, if the fourth person is of the
same gender and number as the third person mentioned, the *nam*
pronoun is used. Mixed gender is treated as masculine. Indicate
when *nam* would be used in the following passages by rewriting
the passage and substituting *nam* for each third person pronoun
in the source that refers to a fourth person. You will need to look
at the context.

1) Mark 16:13

2) Acts 9:17

3) Mark 8:22-26

4) Acts 8:27-31

5) Luke 5:12-14

G. *Introducing participants.* Rewrite the following passage, using these rules of discourse structure: A participant is named within a paragraph by a noun the first time mentioned. After that, within the same paragraph a pronoun is used. If the participant occurs in a second paragraph he is introduced by a noun plus the attributive (this, that, these, or those) the first time mentioned and by pronouns after this introduction.

Mark 11:11-15

And he entered Jerusalem, and went into the temple; and when he had looked around at everything, as it was already late, he went out to Bethany with the twelve.

On the following day, when they came from Bethany, he was hungry. And seeing in the distance a fig tree in leaf, he went to see if he could find anything on it. When he came to it, he found nothing but leaves . . . And he said to it, "May no one ever eat fruit from you again." And his disciples heard it.

And they came to Jerusalem. And he entered the temple and began to drive out those who sold and those who bought in the temple.

H. *Clause connectors.* Rewrite the same passage, keeping the rules given in Section G and adding the following rules: The connector *and* is used only to connect coordinate nouns, noun phrases, or coordinate clauses and never to connect clauses or sentences in sequence. A clause beginning with *when*, referring to time, always follows the main clause that it modifies.

I. *Applying discourse rules.* Using the information in the chart on Mark 8:22-26 on page 233, rewrite the story, using the following rules:

1) Declarative clauses have this structure:
   $\pm$ Comp $\pm$ Pred $\pm$ Obj $\pm$ Loc $\pm$ Subj $\pm$ Time

2) Sentences have from one to five clauses.

3) A quotation fills the object slot.

4) All fillers of the location slot have an obligatory location-marking suffix *-ta*.

5) All fillers of the direct object (DO) slot have an obligatory object-marking suffix = *no.*

6) All fillers of the indirect object (IO) slot have an obligatory suffix *-mu.*

7) All predicates occurring in the final clause of a sentence take an obligatory set of verb margin suffixes indicating person, tense, and mode. The suffix for third person, declarative, past tense is *-kinpo.*

8) Any change of actor is indicated by an obligatory noun as participant and requires a new sentence.

9) A previously introduced participant as goal is indicated by an obligatory pronoun as participant.

10) If two actions in sequence have the same indirect goal, only the first takes an obligatory participant as indirect goal, the second never does.

11) All quotes are direct quotes.

12) Sequential actions within a sentence are connected by *and.*

13) Sentences are not connected by any overt marker within a paragraph.

14) A new paragraph is signalled by a focus on time or actor. In a clause the focus slot precedes the predicate and its complement.

Mark 8:22-26 (NEB)

They arrived at Bethsaida. There the people brought a blind man to Jesus and begged him to touch him. He took the blind man by the hand and led him away out of the village. Then he spat on his eyes, laid his hands upon him, and asked whether he could see anything. The man's sight began to come back, and he said, "I see men; they look like trees, but they are walking about." Jesus laid his hands on his eyes again; he looked hard, and now he was cured so that he saw everything clearly. Then Jesus sent him home, saying, "Do not tell anyone in the village."

MARK 8:22-26

Time	Participants			Action	Comple-ment	Location	Quote
	Actor	Goal–DO	Goal–IO				
	Jesus and disciples			arrived		Bethsaida	
	people	blind*	Jesus	brought		Bethsaida	
	people		Jesus	begged			to touch blind man
	Jesus	blind		took	by hand		
	Jesus	blind		led away		out of village	
	Jesus			spat		on blind's eyes	
	Jesus			laid hands		on blind	
	Jesus		blind	asked			if he (blind) could see anything.
	blind's sight			began to come back			
	blind			said			I see men; they look like trees, but they are walking about.
	Jesus			laid hands	again	on blind's eyes	
	blind			looked	hard		
now	blind			was cured			
	blind	every-thing		saw	clearly		
then	Jesus	blind		sent		to blind's home	
	Jesus		blind	said			Do not tell anyone in village.
	*blind = blind man						

CHAPTER 24

Prominence

TEXT: K. Callow, 1974, chapter 4

ADDITIONAL READING:

Grimes, Joseph E., 1972, *The Thread of Discourse.* Technical Report No. 1, National Science Foundation Grant GS-3180, Ithaca: Cornell University

Sheffler, Margaret, 1969, "Results of Network Diagramming: as applied to the Revision of Mundurukú Mark," *NOT* 32:2-32

Taber, Charles R., 1966, "The Structure of Sango Narrative," *Hartford-Studies in Linguistics,* No. 17, Parts I and II, Hartford, Conn.: The Hartford Seminary Foundation

Wallis, Ethel E., 1971a, "Contrastive Plot Structures of the Four Gospels," *NOT* 40:3-16

Wallis, Ethel E., 1971b, "Discourse Focus in Mezquital Otomi," *NOT* 42:19-21

Wonderly, William, 1968, *Bible Translations for Popular Use,* American Bible Society, 194-96

Prominence "refers to any device whatever which gives certain events, participants, or objects more significance than others in the same context" (K. Callow, 1974, 50).

A. *Thematic prominence.* "The thematic material is material that develops the theme of a discourse, by contrast with background material, which fills out the theme but does not develop it. The theme of a discourse constitutes a progression, called . . . the time-line and the theme-line" (K. Callow, 1974, 53).

Identify the propositions that carry the time-line or the theme-line in each of the following passages. (Follow the steps on page 92 of the text.)

Example: Col. 1:15-20
(God's Son) exactly reveals (Gr.: is the image of) God.
He rules over everything. (He is the first-born of all creation.)
He is (existed) before anything existed.
He maintains all things. (He holds all things together.)
He rules over the church. (He is the head of the body, the church.)
He is supreme (Gr.: beginning).
He is the ruler (Gr.: first-born).

1) Col. 1:21-23

2) Col. 1:24-29

3) Acts 3:1-10

4) Mark 8:22-26

5) John 14:1-7

B. *Thematic function of relative clauses.* "The Greek relative clause has a wide variety of functions. One of these is thematic; that is to say, it carries information that is on the theme-line. An example of this is found in Colossians 1:12, 13: 'Giving thanks unto the Father, *which* hath made us meet . . . *who* hath delivered us . . . .' In this case the relative pronoun, which normally is translated by English *who, which,* does not carry any backgrounding significance whatever; it simply serves as a participant-referent for the clause, and is then better translated by *he, it,* or the appropriate personal pronoun" (K. Callow, 1974, 59, 60).

Study the relative clauses in the following sentences and decide which of them introduce a thematic proposition and which introduce a background proposition. If the proposition is thematic rewrite without using a relative clause.

1) Acts 13:7
He was with the proconsul, Sergius Paulus, a man of intelligence, who summoned Barnabas and Saul and sought to hear the Word of God.

2) Acts 14:3
. . . speaking boldly for the Lord, who bore witness to the word of his grace, granting signs and wonders to be done by their hands.

3) Acts 14:8

Now at Lystra there was a man sitting, who could not use his feet; he was a cripple from birth, who had never walked.

4) Rom. 7:4

Likewise, my brethren, you have died to the law through the body of Christ, so that you may belong to another, to him who has been raised from the dead in order that we may bear fruit to God.

5) 2 Cor. 2:14

Thanks be to God, who in Christ always leads us in triumph, and through us spreads the fragrance of the knowledge of him everywhere.

6) 2 Cor. 8:16, 17

But thanks be to God, who puts the same earnest care for you into the heart of Titus. For he not only accepted our appeal, but being himself very earnest, he is going to you of his own accord.

7) Col. 3:4

When Christ who is our life appears, then you also will appear with him in glory.

8) 1 Thess. 5:9, 10

For God has not destined us for wrath, but to obtain salvation through our Lord Jesus Christ, who died for us so that whether we wake or sleep we might live with him.

9) 1 Thess. 5:24

He who calls you is faithful, and he will do it.

10) 1 Tim. 2:3, 4

This is good, and it is acceptable in the sight of God our Savior, who desires all men to be saved and to come to the knowledge of the truth.

C. *Prominence with focus value.* "Focus is that type of prominence which acts as a spotlight, playing on the thematic material to bring some of it especially to attention. In some languages, focus is an obligatory category and one cannot avoid using it" (K. Callow, 1974, 60).

Study the following and decide what participant, location, or concept is in focus in the passage.

Example: Col. 1:15-20
    Christ is in focus throughout the passage.

1) Eph. 3:1-13

2) Eph. 5:25-33

3) 1 Thess. 1:2-10

4) John 6:25-35

5) Luke 19:41-44

6) 1 Tim. 3:1-7

7) 1 Tim. 4:1-5

8) Heb. 7:1-3

9) Heb. 7:15-19

10) Rev. 21:1-4

D. *Focus of participants.* "Many languages assume that the participant functioning as agent is in focus, and that this is expressed grammatically as the subject of a clause. This creates considerable problems in translation, since Greek could have several different participants all functioning as agents (and sometimes all as grammatical subjects) in the space of one verse. A literal translation here would cause the readers considerable confusion as focus was apparently shifted rapidly from character to character. In Cakchiquel (Guatemala) it is natural to keep one participant in focus for several clauses, and therefore verses sound very unnatural if they switch focus from one participant to another and then back to the first again. In these cases Cakchiquel sometimes uses a passive construction so as to maintain focus on the first participant throughout. An example of this is found in Mark 9:31, 'The Son of man is delivered into the hands of men, and they shall kill him.' Here the Cakchiquel reads, 'I, the Son of man, will be delivered into the hands of men and *I will be killed,*' thus avoiding introducing 'they' as grammatical subject of 'will kill' " (K. Callow, 1974, 62).

Rewrite the following so that only the one participant in focus (the italicized) occurs as the subject of the clause. The other participants will have to occupy other slots in the clause.

Example: Mark 10:1-10

> And he left there and went to the region of Judea . . . he taught them. And Pharisees came up and in order to test him asked, ". . . ." He answered them, ". . . ." And in the house the disciples asked him again about the matter.
>
> And he left there and went to the region of Judea . . . he taught them. And he was asked by the Pharisees who came up to him in order to test him asking, ". . . ." He answered them, ". . . ." Again in the house he was asked by his disciples about the matter.

1) Mark 14:10, 11

> Then *Judas* Iscariot, who was one of the twelve, went to the chief priests in order to betray him to them. And when they heard it they were glad, and promised to give him money. And he sought an opportunity to betray him.

2) Mark 14:72

> And immediately the cock crowed a second time. And *Peter* remembered how Jesus had said to him . . . . And he broke down and wept.

3) Luke 4:42, 43

> And when it was day *he* (Jesus) departed and went into a lonely place. And the people sought him and came to him, and would have kept him from leaving them; but he said to them . . . .

4) Acts 8:26-31

> But an angel of the Lord said to *Philip*, "Rise and go toward the south . . . ." And he rose and went. And behold, an Ethiopian . . . was returning; seated in his chariot, he was reading the prophet Isaiah. And the Spirit said to Philip, "Go . . . ." So Philip ran to him, and heard him reading Isaiah . . . and asked, ". . . ." And he said, ". . . ." And he invited Philip to come up and sit with him.

CHAPTER 25

Information Load

TEXT: K. Callow, 1974, chapter 5

ADDITIONAL READING:

Duff, Martha, 1973, "Contrastive Features of Written and Oral Texts in Amuesha," *NOT* 50:2-13

Kingston, Peter L. E., 1973, "Repetition as a Feature of Discourse Structure in Mamainde," *NOT* 50:13-22

Larson, Mildred L., 1969, "Making Explicit Information Implicit," *NOT* 33:15-20

Nida, 1964, 120-44

Nida and Taber, 1969, 163-68

Wonderly, William, 1968, *Bible Translations for Popular Use*, The American Bible Society, 182-94

A. *Known and new information.* Different languages present information at a different rate. A translation should communicate biblical information at a rate within the normal patterns of the receptor language.

Identify the old and new information in the following passage by underlining the new information (Things and Events) in red and the old information in blue.

Luke 10:30-35

[30]A man was going down from Jerusalem to Jericho and he fell among robbers, who stripped him and beat him, and departed, leaving him half-dead. [31]Now by chance a priest was going down that road; and when he saw him he passed by on the other side. [32]So likewise a Levite, when he came to the place and saw him, passed by on the other side. [33]But a

Samaritan, as he journeyed, came to where he was; and when he saw him, he had compassion, [34]and went to him and bound up his wounds, pouring on oil and wine; then he set him on his own beast and brought him to an inn, and took care of him. [35]And the next day he took out two denarii and gave them to the innkeeper.

B. *Linking new to known information in discourse.* The first time a Thing or Event is mentioned new information is being introduced. Each time it is referred to again it is considered old information. In the passages below look for ways old information is signaled by doing the following:

a) Take the first participant introduced and list the ways it is referred to in all further references. Then take the second participant introduced and do the same. In this way study how participants are referred to when newly introduced (new information) and how they are referred to when again mentioned subsequently in the text.

b) List the Events that occur in the text in order. See if any Event is referred to more than once. The first time it will be new information. When it is referred to again it will be old information. Does the form used differ?

First look for the new and old information and how it is signaled in the RSV. Then do the same with the passage in the language given below.

1) John 1:35-44
Tepehua: [35]The next day again John was standing with two of his men. [36]And he again saw Jesus where he was coming and said to them, "Look at that man who is going to be like God's lamb." [37]And those two of John's when they heard what he said, well, immediately they followed Jesus. [38]And when Jesus turned around he saw those who were following him. He said to them, "What are you hunting for?" And they said to him, "Rabbi, where do you live?" Rabbi means teacher. [39]Well, he said to them, "Come. You will see where I live." And they went with him. They saw where he lived. Well, that day they stayed there with him, since it was about four in the afternoon. [40]And those two who heard John's words and followed Jesus, well, one was called Andrew. He was the younger brother of Simon Peter.

⁴¹Well, Andrew immediately found his real brother who was called Simon. And he said to his brother, "We have found the Messiah. That means we have found the Christ, the one of whom it was said that God would send him here." ⁴²And immediately he took him to where Jesus was. When Jesus saw him he said to him, "You are Simon. You are the son of Jonas. You will be called Cephas." Cephas and Peter mean rock. ⁴³When the next day came, Jesus said that he was going to the land of Galilee. There he came across the one who was called Philip. And he said to him that he should follow him. ⁴⁴Philip lived in the town of Bethsaida. It was the land of Andrew and Peter.

2) Acts 1:21-24

Aguaruna: ²¹"Because it says like that, we ought to look for another, 'Who it ought to be,' saying. ²²It should be one who beginning when John baptized Jesus, always was with Jesus, being one who was left by him when he went to heaven. When he is thus, with him we can tell 'Jesus truly rose,' saying." ²³When Peter said that, they said, "Let it be Joseph Barabbas, called Justus." When they said, others speaking said, "Let it be Matthias." ²⁴When they said that, they prayed to God, "Lord, you see the heart of each one. You being thus, 'who is it' you choose, 'It is he,' saying."

3) Mark 7:31-35

Waffa: ³¹Jesus returned and came again from the town called Tyre, passed through the town called Sidon, passed through the big town called Decapolis and came and sat on the bank of Lake Galilee. ³²He sat, and the friends of a man who was deaf and could not talk got him and went to Jesus. They went, and strongly asked Jesus to touch him. ³³When they had asked him, Jesus . . . .

C. *Preview and summary.* Preview and summary are also used to slow down the information load. Study the following passages and (1) identify any propositions whose function seems to be to provide a preview or a summary; (2) if any of the following passages do not have a preview or summary proposition suggest a possible wording for such a proposition for the passage.

1) Matt. 1:18-25

2) Matt. 4:1-11

3) Matt. 9:1-8

4) Rom. 8:1-17

5) 1 Cor. 13

D. *Reducing the rate of information.* The text (K. Callow, 1974, 84, 85) suggests that there are the following ways in which the receptor language may adjust the information load so as to have a slower flow of new information.

a) Splitting an original construction into smaller units using repetition as linkage.

b) Splitting an original construction into smaller units using implied information as linkage.

c) Splitting an original construction into smaller units in such a way that no additional linkage is needed.

d) Splitting an original construction into more units using semantically neutral words.

Following each passage given below is a back-translation from a specific language. Identify any occurrences of the above in the back-translation.

Example: Rom. 6:23
For the wages of sin is death.
Huisteco: Because the one who works for sin, he will be paid for his work. The payment of his work will be that he will be lost eternally.
Answer: a

1) Luke 15:12
Father, give me the share of property that falls to me.

Kasem:
Father, take your possessions and divide, result you give me my share.

2) Matt. 8:4
See that you say nothing to anyone; show yourself to the priest, and offer the gift that Moses commanded, for a proof to the people.

Shipibo:

See that you tell no one. Go your way to show yourself to the priest. So that they may know that you are healed, offer the gift that Moses commanded.

3) Luke 10:31

Now by chance a priest was going down that road.

Kasem:

There was a certain priest, he got up and came down that road.

4) Acts 1:21, 22

So one of the men who have accompanied us during all the time that the Lord Jesus went in and out among us . . . must become with us a witness to his resurrection.

Aguaruna:

Because it says like that, we ought to look for another, "Who it ought to be," saying. It should be one who always was with Jesus . . . When he is thus, with him we can tell, "Jesus truly rose," saying.

5) John 2:11

This, the first of his signs, Jesus did at Cana in Galilee, and manifested his glory; and his disciples believed in him.

Tepehua:

This thing to be marvelled at Jesus did in the town of Cana in the land of Galilee. That is the first thing to be marvelled at that Jesus did. In that way he showed to the people his power. At that time, then, his disciples believed on Jesus more.

6) John 2:9

When the steward of the feast tasted the water now become wine, and did not know where it came from (though the servants who had drawn the water knew), the steward of the feast called the bridegroom.

Totonac:

And the chief tasted it, and it was wine, and he didn't know that it had been water and that the water had been changed to wine. Only the servants knew because they had put the water into water pots.

7) John 3:1
Now there was a man of the Pharisees, named Nicodemus, a ruler of the Jews.

Ojitlan Chinantec:
A man was named Nicodemus. He believed according to the law of the Pharisee people. And he was a head man of the Jews.

8) John 3:15
that whoever believes in him may have eternal life

Tepehua:
When I will have been thus, all who will have confidence in me won't be lost. They will have life forever up in heaven.

9) John 5:2
Now there is in Jerusalem by the sheep gate a pool, in Hebrew called Bethzatha, which has five porticoes.

Lalana Chinantec:
In Jerusalem there is a large hole containing water where people bathe. It is near the gate in the wall which goes around the outside of town which is called the gate of sheep. They call the hole which contains water Bethzatha in the Hebrew language. There were five porches along the water.

E. *Expected information.* There is certain information that is only implied in the Greek but which may be expected in the receptor language and therefore needs to be added in a given translation if the translation is to sound natural. "In many West African languages . . . any motion that took place must be stated. In the story of Moses in the bulrushes, Exodus 2:3, 'she took for him an ark . . . and put the child therein; and she laid it in the flags by the river's brink.' Motion is implied in the last clause of the verse: Moses' mother had to go to the river in order to leave the child there. This is clear, were proof needed, from vv. 7 and

8. Moses' sister said, 'Shall I *go* and call to thee a nurse . . .?' She then *went* and called the child's mother. Thus it is obvious that their home was not right at the water's edge — motion was involved. In Kasem, motion is not normally implied, but stated, so the last clause of the verse becomes 'she *went* to the river's brink and laid it in the flags.' This is not only more natural, and avoids confusion; it also spreads out the information in a more acceptable way. To attach both 'in the flags' and 'by the river's brink' to the single verb 'laid' would be too heavy an information load in Kasem" (K. Callow, 1974, 87).

In each of the following passages look for events that are implied in the source language and which may need to be made explicit in the receptor language.

1) Matt. 2:7, 8, 12

2) Matt. 4:1, 2

3) Matt. 9:9, 10

4) Mark 3:6

5) John 2:9, 10

6) Acts 20:5

7) Acts 24:24

8) Matt. 18:21